FIONA VELLA • OLIVER GATT

BIZarRE
MALTA

mysterious • quirky • wonderful

BDL Publishing

© Book Distributors Limited, Malta
www.bdlbooks.com
info@bdlbooks.com
www.fb.com/BDLBooks

First edition, 2018

BIZaRRE MALTA

mysterious • quirky • wonderful

Text by Fiona Vella & Oliver Gatt
with contributions by Michael Cassar

Photography by © Oliver Gatt
Typesetting and design by Book Distributors Limited

Bizarre Malta on facebook
www.fb.com/bizarremalta

ISBN: 978-99957-99-11-3

Printed by Gutenberg Press, Ħal Tarxien

FIONA VELLA • OLIVER GATT

BIZARRE MALTA

mysterious • quirky • wonderful

BDL Publishing

FIONA VELLA • OLIVER GATT

BIZARRE
MALTA

mysterious • quirky • wonderful

NOTE TO READER

The fact that a location or artefact is described in this book does not mean that it is necessarily possible or safe for you to visit it. Please be advised that visiting and exploring old, abandoned and out-of-the-way sites can be in itself hazardous.

A number of sites mentioned in this book are private property, or are surrounded by private property. Avoid trespassing at all times. Readers seeking to visit sites and locations mentioned in this book do so at their own risk and at their own liability to third party property. Your use of this book indicates your assumption of risk, and is an acknowledgement of your own sole responsibility for your safety whilst visiting and exploring these sites. The authors, editors and publishers of this book disclaim any liability whatsoever.

Acknowledgements

Aaron Abela, Nicholas Abela, Anthony Abela Medici, Saviour Sam Agius, Edward Attard, Robert Aquilina, Godwin Azzopardi, Ivan A. Bondin, Giovanni Bonello, Eman Bonnici, John J. Borg, Joseph Brincat, Michael Buhagiar, Narcy Calamatta, David Camilleri, Maroma Camilleri, Ray Camilleri, Debbie Caruana Dingli, Michael Cassar, Petra Coppini, Alfredo Cutajar, Denis Darmanin, Nicholas De Gabriele, Nicholas de Piro, Ian Ellis, Charles J. Farrugia, Natalino Fenech, Albert Ganado, Anthony Gatt, Joseph F. Grima, Aline Larsberg, Martin Micallef, Ray Polidano, Edward J. Said, Stephen Said, Louis J. Scerri, Karl Scicluna, Joseph Schirò, Paul Spiteri Lucas, Conrad Thake, Robert Thake, Paul and Gino Trapani Galea Feriol, Josephine Tyndale Biscoe, Maurizio Urso, Jason Vella, Mark Vella, Roderick Vella, Margareth Verbakel, Gordon Weston, William Zammit.

CONTENTS

8

FOREWORD

Giovanni Bonello

Hand in hand with Fiona Vella and Oliver Gatt we walk through quite untrodden paths. Most visitors and other curious travellers usually herd and stop at the tourist traps, certified as such by the hundreds of thousands who did it before. The weight of repetition bestows credence upon places and validates their claims to high visibility. This book sets out to be totally different – it beckons readers in the opposite direction. It tells us: be the first. It tells us: there are still corners tucked away in the fold of the islands' geography or in the nooks of their history where the attraction lies not in the spectacular, in high creative art, in objects that evoke crucial moments in history, but in neglected, mysterious, weird, inexplicable buildings, or places, or phenomena. The façade of a village house damascened in seashells – Renzo Piano it ain't, but nonetheless it is a spectacular monument to single-mindedness and the ego's craving to stand out as different.

Such a 'guide book' has never been done before, certainly not on the systematic scale that the authors have undertaken in this volume. The closest was the easier and the more obvious: a ramble through the spooky abodes of ghosts, apparitions, spectres, and the paranormal, which still seem to hold interest for some. Frankly, I have little time for anything that requires me to suspend both belief and disbelief. The authors are here on far surer, though equally intriguing, grounds. They introduce the realm of the opaque, the paradoxical, the irrational, the absurd, the impervious. I wonder why they left the law courts out.

Gatt and Vella do it in a pleasant, engaging way, with flair, backed up by compacted research. They have an eye for a good story. Though some narratives derived from old legends are included, their primary inspiration lies in the disciplines of history, rather than the blandishments of literature. At the core of each yarn lie facts, not creativity. It is that central fact, sometimes filtered through centuries of amnesia, distortion, perhaps denial or wishful thinking, that provides the cohesive thread that runs through most of these chapters.

Is everything contained in this volume certified, monolithic truth? That, in itself, would be something extraordinarily bizarre. I would not make that claim for any book, be it history, science, philosophy, even mathematics; except, perhaps, for autobiographies which relentlessly embrace nothing but the truth. I believe that the authors have really striven to remain as close as possible to the boundaries of serious research. When they report that de Valette beheaded all Turkish prisoners in the Great Siege, to use their heads as cannon balls, they are recounting a 'fact' mentioned in old documents: But could it be true? A human head would have left the cannon shaft as creamy pap the instant it was subjected to the power of exploding gunpowder. It is, however, a newsworthy, if nauseatingly macabre story, hinged to reputable written 'evidence'. And anyway if, occasionally, in the sources the authors have relied on, there is a slip here and a minor fall there, this all adds to the frisson of the narrative. This is not principally a fun book, but it is allowed to be a fun book once in a while.

The authors judiciously selected both man-made objects of interest and those where nature did its own thing and neglected to tell us why. What the two have in common is their ability to arouse curiosity, or awe, or disbelief, or rejection, or fear – sometimes a mixture of two or more. Here are mostly narratives with a beginning, a progress, and with a question for an answer. Often the suspense does not end with a Hitchcock denouement, the mystery looms at the beginning of the quest, and mystery still gnaws at its end. This lack of closure is probably more common in the enigmas conjured by nature than in the man-made imbroglios.

I am not aware whether this book will be the beginning of a series. There are still other mysteries and baffling phenomena out there waiting to be recorded and shared with the inquisitive. Perhaps the success of this volume will encourage the authors to cast their dragnet further still. They have opted for the umbrella title of 'Bizarre', which fits quite well all the stories in this book. But bizarre, in Malta, is not a rare commodity at all. Often it is the new normal.

1

EVERLASTING AWE

The Face in the Cliffs at Dwejra, Gozo

Dwejra area in Gozo never fails to amaze. The landlocked 'Inland Sea', the isolated 'Fungus Rock', the Punic-Roman sanctuary at Ras il-Wardija further afield, and, until recently, the geological gem known as the Azure Window are all concentrated in one short stretch of coast in western Gozo. A boat trip which leaves from the Inland Sea, goes through a tunnel in the cliffs and out to the open sea will reveal a huge gaping face chiselled in the cliffs by the natural elements. The face looks out at the site where the Azure Window natural arch stood until 8 March 2017 and seems to be frozen in shock at its absence, a sentiment shared by many Maltese and Gozitans.

Palazzo Falson, Mdina.

2

UNDER LOCK AND KEY

The Palazzo Falson Chastity Belt, Mdina

For several centuries, it was believed that medieval married women were forced to wear metal chastity belts to prevent them from having sexual intercourse with other men while their husbands were away from home. These chastity belts would lock up the female genitalia in metal girdles, leaving only enough space for the basic natural daily needs. To ensure marital fidelity, the husband would take away the lock's key with him and his wife would be freed from this device only on his return.

Chastity belts exhibited in museums or in personal collections often created a sense of shock and disgust at such a horrifying and extreme method of enforcing fidelity. Yet recent academic studies about these misogynistic tools are starting to reveal that chastity belts may have never been really worn by women after all. Clearly, it was hardly possible for a woman to survive even a few days with such a device on, both owing to the wounds, pain, and discomfort that it would have inflicted and also the serious hygiene and health consequences which it would give rise to. Detailed research is showing that evidence related to chastity belts is largely anecdotal or found in burlesque fiction, thereby indicating that this device was merely a fictitious invention. Possibly this myth was meant to attribute a barbaric character to the Middle Ages or was simply a tasteless joke.

However, E.J. Dingwall in *The Girdle of Chastity* (London, 1931) alleges that chastity belts were invented in Italy around 1400 and were in actual use, albeit rarely, right into the twentieth century. Their use during the Renaissance, however, is largely anecdotal or found only in satirical fiction. It is probable that the great majority of existent examples were whimsically crafted in the eighteenth and nineteenth centuries.

The first written evidence of a chastity belt was recorded by Keyser von Eichstad, a retired soldier who compiled a manuscript in 1405 about the art of war and military equipment.

The Palazzo Falson chastity belt. Another, more plausible, use for the chastity belt seems to have been that of protecting women from being raped by the enemy. Given that wearing the belt for a period longer than a day or two would have resulted in serious discomfort, not to mention infection, the belt would have functioned like armour if worn briefly for travelling or in dangerous situations. (courtesy: Palazzo Falson Historic House Museum, Mdina)

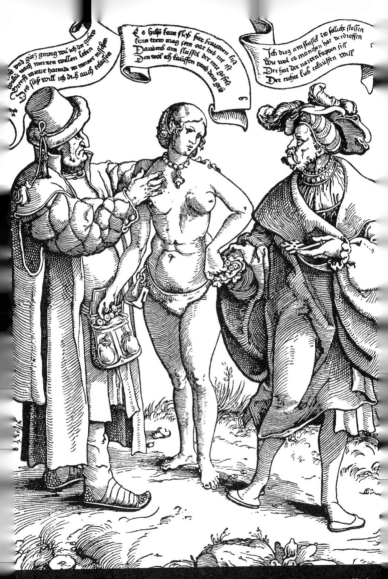

A sixteenth-century German satirical woodcut showing the old husband offering his young wife money to encourage her to agree to wear the chastity belt he made her wear, while she intends to use that money to buy herself a new key.

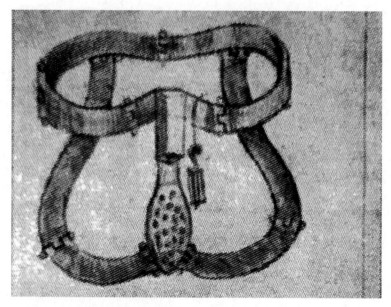

A sketch of a chastity belt from *Bellifortis*, a fully illustrated manual of military technology by Konrad Kyeser published in 1405.

In his book *Bellifortis*, von Eichstad included a drawing of a chastity belt with the inscription (translated from Latin): 'Breeches of hard Florentine iron that are closed at the front'. This chastity belt was worn by the women of Florence as a method of preventing rape.

In 1996, an exhibit at the British Museum which was believed to be a medieval chastity belt was removed after it was found out to be fake and dating only to between the eighteenth and the nineteenth century. One can view a chastity belt at Palazzo Falson, a thirteenth-century palace in Mdina which was the home of Captain Olof Frederick Gollcher, OBE (1889–1962). An artist, a scholar, and a philanthropist, Gollcher was also an avid collector of artistic and historical objects.

3

A REPOSITORY OF UNWANTED NEWBORNS

La Ruota, Rabat

The large building, adjacent to St Francis church in the narrow Hospital Street, Rabat (Malta), today houses the National Archives but originally it served as a hospital. The third arched feature on the left side from the main doorway of its elegant façade in former times housed a revolving contraption known as *la ruota* (the wheel) which made it possible for unwanted babies to be left anonymously.

The enclosed wooden aperture of the *ruota* on Hospital Street, Rabat, now home to the National Archives of Malta.

In use since at least 1372, the hospital named after St Francis is Malta's earliest hospital, and it offered care to the poor and the sick thanks to funding by the Church. In 1433, its administration was transferred to the Universitas (the local municipality) and its name was changed to Santo Spirito Hospital. This name was commonly used by medieval hospitals in Europe which specialized in looking after foundlings and pregnant mothers.

In 1574, during his visit to the hospital, Mgr Pietro Dusina, the first General Inquisitor and Apostolic Delegate of the Maltese Islands, laid down detailed rules concerning the hospital's administration which included the reception and care given to foundlings and the submission of an annual report to the bishop. A 1599 report indicates that eight foundlings were being received at this hospital annually.

La ruota is recorded at least in 1615. It consisted of a narrow window which led to a revolving wooden cot wherein babies could be placed safely and anonymously. When turned, it rang a bell in the process. Such infants would then belong to the state.

It is believed that the Maltese surname Spiteri derived from the Italian word *Ospitalieri* (Hospitallers) which was sometimes given to the illegitimate children who were left at *la ruota* during the rule of the Order of St John. The surname is, however, recorded locally before 1530. With the arrival of the Order in Malta, foundling care services were also provided in other areas, including the Birgu *Sacra Infermeria*.

In his study 'Social services for unwed mothers and their children', Charles Savona-Ventura states that a number of wet-nurses were employed to nurture these foundlings. At the age of 8, the children were then transferred to *conservatori*: the boys to Fort Ricasoli and apprenticed to several artisans until the age of 16 years, while the girls were taught a handicraft until the age of 20 years.

A life-size figure of a woman and her baby with a replica of the Rabat foundling wheel at the Mdina Dungeons museum in Mdina. (courtesy: Mdina Dungeons)

For centuries, prostitution was a flourishing concern in Malta, resulting in many unwanted pregnancies. Children born out of wedlock were considered a shame and an inconvenience and the *ruota* partly resolved such 'problems'. The Victorian era saw a changing culture which emphasized a more prurient attitude towards sex.

This resulted in a drop in the number of illegitimate children as hasty marriages were arranged to fix such 'accidents' while most unmarried mothers sought to deliver their babies in hospitals. With the *ruota* being abolished in the late nineteenth century, some newborns were abandoned in the streets and in churches. Those foundlings were taken to the police and placed in the care of orphan asylums.

The aperture of the *ruota* in Hospital Street features the curved wooden flank of the original contraption.

4

A MYSTICAL TOWER

Xlejli Tower, Palazzo Dorell and Gardens, Gudja

Close to the crossroads which lead to Ħal Tarxien, Ħal Għaxaq, Gudja, and Ħal Luqa, there is the imposing landmark of Palazzo Dorell, also known as Villa Bettina, whose quirky cylindrical Xlejli Tower immediately steals the spotlight.

The date of the tower's construction is not known but most sources agree that it was intended as a watchtower and not for defensive purposes. A book printed in 1570 is said to date it to the twelfth or the thirteenth century whereas Louis de Boisgelin, the historian of the Order of St John writing in 1804, suggests that it could even go back to Roman or medieval times. He even goes on to say that an urn full of Roman copper medals had been found at the tower. Could he be referring to an older tower and not to Xlejli?

In *5000 Years of Architecture in Malta*, Leonard Mahoney states that Xlejli Tower was built around an old watchtower, thereby indicating the presence of an earlier structure.

Apparently, the old tower found itself incorporated in the walled gardens of Palazzo Dorell when this luxurious country house was built close by. When *Marchesa* Bettina Dorell (Elisabetta Moscati Sceberras Dorell Falzon), a member of one of Malta's richest noble families, became the owner of this property, the residence was turned into an enchanting spot wherein she could entertain her visitors.

The *marchesa* had previously resided at the court of Naples as lady-of-honour to Queen Maria Carolina of Naples, the sister of Queen Marie-Antoinette of France. Besides embellishing the house with refined taste, the *marchesa* created a fantastic environment in the gardens. This included a temple-like structure, a grotto of coloured stones and shells, an octagonal gazebo, a collection of strange beasts and animals worked in stone, and a vaulted hermitage designed to look like a monk's cell. This hermitage consists of two round structures that look like large Maltese *giren* or corbelled stone huts. One of these 'huts' is built of huge masonry blocks and roofed over with a circular assemblage of tightly-fitting blocks, each measuring *circa* 1.5 metres, that converge in the centre to an octagonal keystone with a hole at its centre. This arrangement is also reflected in the flooring of the hut. Interestingly, there

Opposite: One of the peacocks that live in the palazzo's garden flies past the rustic tower. Below: Palazzo Dorell, also known as Villa Bettina, with Xlejli Tower on the left showing behind the façade.

Above: The larger of the two stone huts (the monk's cell) in the garden of Palazzo Dorell. Opposite: The interior of the 'monk's cell' showing the stone statue of the contemplative monk from Siena and the massive stones projecting from the ambulatory wall.

is a space of about 60 cm between the double outside walls that functions as an ambulatory around the entire cell. The structure is crowned with vertically-placed unworked stones of considerable dimensions that also flank the doorway endowing the building with a mystical aura. In the book *Splendor of Malta*, Shirley Jackewicz Johnston claims that this hermitage was dedicated to a friar from Siena. A stone statue of this monk in a contemplative stance and surrounded by scrolls is the focal point of this circular space. Opposite is a small table with candlesticks all worked in stone.

A Latin inscription over the doorway reads:

Nemo meas miretur aedes: palatium hic habito amplissimum, cum eternos orci carcero et aeternas coeli mansiones cogito.

The Latin inscription over the entrance to the larger stone hut.

'No one admires my temple, this enormous palace where I live enclosed with the underworld for eternity and thinking about eternal dwellings in the heavens.'

The *marchesa* also transformed the old lookout tower into an exclusive folly which she named 'Xlejli', literally meaning 'tacked together' for the technique used to combine a mixture of rough stones and dark pieces of glass.

The ruined appearance of the tower evoked a sense of nostalgia, offering the *marchesa* the opportunity to create a unique masterpiece to amuse her visitors. She restored and decorated its three circular rooms which were set on top of each other and could be accessed by an external spiral staircase. All the internal walls were richly frescoed, the beams and ceilings wonderfully painted with bands, garlands, shells, birds, and floral motifs in rich colours.

The first room is extravagantly arrayed with a large circular table set up with dishes of food, bread, fruit, bottles, and wine goblets, all worked in stone. The second-storey

Top: The monk's cell with the ambulatory to the right.
Above: The rear of the larger stone hut.

Above: Internal view of the smaller of the two huts showing the stonework of the ceiling. Below: The garden path decorated with curious stone-carved animal figures.

room is dominated by two statues representing the female Greek poet Sappho of Lesbos and the Roman virgin goddess Vesta facing each other. The walls are hung with multicoloured chintz; on the plinth in the centre there once stood another statue.

The walls of the third and loftiest room are an all-round canvas depicting a continuous strange and imaginary landscape inhabited by what look like knights and soldiers,

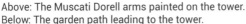

Above: The Muscati Dorell arms painted on the tower.
Below: The garden path leading to the tower.

The table on the first floor of the tower set with fruit, meat, bread, and wine goblets, all worked in stone and painted. Opposite, above: The ceiling over the fruit table on the first floor of Xlejli Tower. Opposite, below: Detail of the 'food table'.

Detail of the base of the tower with pieces of dark glass inserted in the wall.

as well as country folk from different eras amid churches, lakes, walled cities, and follies, some of which bear some semblance to Maltese scenes. Curiously enough, Xlejli Tower itself is also represented in between the doors and their flanking *trompe l'oeil*.

Those who dare climb up to the top of the vertiginous windy staircase can enjoy extensive views of the island, the best of which being those of Marsaxlokk Harbour. From atop this tower, one can easily imagine the *marchesa* watching Napoleon landing his massive armada of over 400 ships in the southeastern harbour.

Napoleon is believed to have called at Palazzo Dorell during his 12-day stay in Malta before embarking on his Egyptian campaign. Later, when the British ousted the French, Bettina's palace became the headquarters for Brigadier General Thomas Graham whose guests included Lord Nelson and

The second floor of the tower with two statues representing the female Greek poet Sappho of Lesbos and the Roman virgin goddess Vesta facing each other.

Above: The ceiling on the second floor of the tower with decorated bands, birds, and garlands. Below: The third-floor ceiling of the tower folly.

A telescope stands in the centre of the third room of the tower. The walls are decorated with imaginary scenes resembling Maltese landscapes.

Above: Detail from the mural on the top floor showing a hilltop fortress.
Below: Another detail showing country folk, fishermen, and churches.

'Changing Faces' – The curious motif on the ceiling of the house just before entering the garden which, when turned upside down, reveals a second face.

Emma Hamilton and her husband, Sir William Hamilton, the British ambassador to the Kingdom of Naples. Lord Byron also enjoyed the gardens and its peculiar structures when he visited Malta in 1809.

Today the palace is a private residence and Xlejli Tower is not open to the public. Yet, its romantic presence from afar still succeeds to conjure fanciful ideas of myths and legends. The palace is scheduled at Grade 1 by the Planning Authority and listed on the National Inventory of the Cultural Property of the Maltese Islands (NICPMI).

5

A CRYPT OF MUMMIFIED FRIARS

The Capuchin Crypt, Floriana

Driving past the Floriana Health Centre in F.S. Fenech Street, one will reach a small square which is a dead end where the Capuchins' convent is located. Today this building might look quite ordinary, but in the old days, visitors sought it out to experience a macabre spectacle of mummified friars.

The crypt which housed these mummies was dug in solid rock beneath the convent between 1725 and 1730. The project was the idea of Fr Ġużepp Grech and it was funded by Grand Master Anton Manoel de Vilhena. Twenty niches were hollowed out in the walls of the crypt to hold standing mummies of friars.

The exhibitions of mummified friars and decorations with human bones were then a custom of the Capuchin Order. The friars were believed to know a secret embalming process which took a whole year to complete. When a friar passed away, his corpse was taken into a room in the crypt where it was disembowelled and left in a heated chamber with a perforated floor until it dried out. The dehydrated corpse would then be dressed in its friar attire and chained in an upright position in the niche where it was left to decay. An inscription with the deceased's name and date of death identified the friar. Once the mummy collapsed in its niche, the bones would be gathered and taken away to be nailed upon the walls of the

Above: A Capuchin friar in the crypt from a nineteenth-century engraving. (courtesy: Albert Ganado) Below: Some vacant cavities in the Capuchin crypt where the mummified friars used to hang. Opposite: A modern reconstruction of what a mummified friar would have looked like. (photos: Fiona Vella)

crypt as a sort of decoration. The skulls were arranged in rows along the ceiling.

Many people visited this crypt when it was opened once a year on 2 November to celebrate requiem masses in the vault. Foreign visitors described the place as horrific and disgusting and they claimed that the surviving friars who accompanied them in the crypt admitted that they looked forward to joining their deceased brothers in this underground resting place once they passed away. For locals, this crypt was a place of devotion; on that day, the corpses would be adorned with flowers.

On 5 April 1942, during the Second World War, the church and the convent were bombed and destroyed. Ġużeppi Borg from Ħaż-Żabbar died in this crypt on that day when he was buried beneath the rubble. The crypt was eventually restored by Fr Franġisku Azzopardi and reopened to the public by Provincial Fr Ewsebju Darmanin on 31 October 1979.

British officers being shown around the Capuchin crypt in Floriana, nineteenth-century engraving. (courtesy: Albert Ganado)

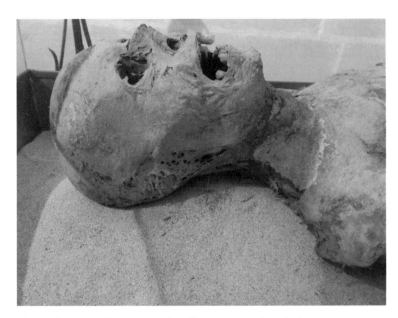

Above: The Capuchin's secret embalming process took a whole year to complete. (photo: Fiona Vella) Below: The church and convent of the Capuchin Order in Floriana.

A few skulls and bones still decorate the walls of the crypt. (photo: Fiona Vella)

Nowadays, the niches are empty, except for one of them which holds a faithful fibreglass reproduction of a mummified friar. Nevertheless, visitors may still see two mummies resting in glass cases. One of them is headless and its identity is unknown. The other belongs to Fra Crispin Zammit, a charitable and pious friar from Gozo who died on 11 March 1867. His mummy was believed to have miraculous powers and several people implored its help.

Although the crypt today is devoid of other human remains except for a few human bones and skulls affixed to a wall and exhibited in a showcase, the place is still rather scary and chilling. A copy of a watercolour painting hanging in this crypt shows the niches still full of decaying mummies, while a photo shows Fra Crispin's ghastly mummy drooping in its niche in tattered clothes.

6

A FATEFUL SANCTUARY
Filfla

The remote islet of Filfla, located 5 km away from the southern coast of Malta, may appear insignificant to the modern eye. However, this small rocky platform has a long and interesting history that is often enhanced with myths and legends. In ancient times, Filfla might have been considered sacred and this could have influenced the construction of the two prehistoric temples of Ħaġar Qim and Mnajdra, both of which have a direct view of it.

A very long time ago, a cataclysmic event separated this island from the mainland, leaving it and whatever lived on it to their own destiny. Endemic species developed in this isolation, including a black lizard with green or blue spots. Growing up to 30 cm in length, this lizard is known as *Podarcis filfolensis filfolensis* and is larger than the lizards found on the Maltese Islands. For many years, it was erroneously believed to be a species with two tails.

Old maps show a church on Filfla. However, according to John Joseph Borg, senior curator at the National Museum of Natural History, this church was only a cave with a wall constructed in front of it. Possibly this structure was financed by a man who had survived a terrible storm in 1343 by finding refuge on the islet. Fishermen used to stop at Filfla to hear mass

Johann Conrad Probst, *Karte von Denen INSELN MALTA COMINO und GOZO* (1798). Filfla is given as an inset map with all the details saying that there is a lighthouse, a small church with living accommodation, and a small fort. It was probably just one building incorporating all these features. (courtesy: Joseph Schirò)

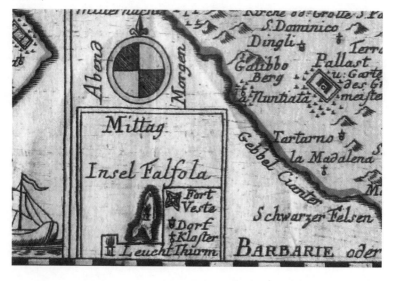

A rare pre-1910 photograph of Filfla showing a distinctly different profile to the one we see today. (photo: A.J. Zammit)

at this church. However, in 1575, during Mgr Pietro Dusina's pastoral visit, a parish priest requested the desecration of this church since he was often finding it difficult to reach the island in rough seas. Since the island was so secluded, he had to carry with him all the required items each time he went to celebrate mass, including a triptych painting known as the *Madonna ta' Filfla*. His demand was accepted and no more masses were celebrated in the church. The triptych painting was taken to Żurrieq parish church, where it can still be admired. Eventually, this church was destroyed during an earthquake in 1856.

Filfla, so close to land and yet so far, has often served as a providential location. Fishermen who found themselves in difficulty could land there until help arrived or the sea calmed down. During the 1813 plague, this islet acted as a sanctuary for Ġanni Attard and his family who went to live there until the epidemic ended. A relative provided them with food and provisions from time to time. During the Second World War,

After 200 years of being used for target practice, Filfla was declared a nature reserve and it became prohibited to land on the islet or to fish or dive close to it.

a German pilot ended in the sea near Filfla after his warplane was shot down. He swam to the islet and was lucky enough to be saved by a comrade who took him away safe and sound. In the old days, Filfla also served as a haven for pirates. Its high cliffs were ideal to hide their vessels, whilst a fresh water spring helped them to replenish themselves with a much-

Filfla from the south (open-sea side) showing the cliff-face destroyed by relentless bombing.

Bomb fragments found on the surface of Filfla. (courtesy: John J. Borg)

needed resource. In 1761, the Order of St John unsuccessfully attempted to destroy this water source. Sadly, the British Forces succeeded to do this later on.

The name 'Filfla' has its roots in the Arabic word *filfel*, meaning 'chili pepper', possibly due to the shape it once had. Part of the island sank during the 1856 earthquake. Yet its original mass was mainly lost because the British used the islet as a target practice area for over 200 years. In the 1970s these bombings were prohibited, but 10 years later, Navy officials exploded some bombs which they found on Filfla, resulting in more damage.

This destruction not only shattered the rocks but also killed and distressed the flora and fauna on the islet. Wild rabbits which were let loose on Filfla for hunting purposes could still be seen until the nineteenth century but none are left today. In 1988, Filfla was declared a natural reserve and it became prohibited to land on the islet or to fish or dive close to it. Since then life has slowly returned to the island, particularly a large colony of storm petrels. Nonetheless, bombs are still present both on land and in the surrounding sea.

A deed of land division registered by the affluent Testaferrata family in the records of Notary Cristoforo Frendo of 20 July 1818 shows some land on Filfla, then known as 'Fulfula', was to be inherited by the heirs of Marquis Don Pandolfo Testaferrata. Today, Filfla is government property. Access to it is possible only for research and educational purposes.

Two separate reported incidents of shells fired from British ships, aimed at Filfla during military practice in 1954, missed their target and landed in fields in the limits of Il-Kunċizzjoni, limits of Mġarr, and at Qrendi. The missiles exploded on impact, leaving craters and causing damage to rubble walls. Nobody was injured during these incidents.

7

A SUBTERRANEAN CAVERN OF
UNKNOWN WATER DEPTHS
Ħarq Ħammiem Cave, St George's Bay, St Julian's

The area around St George's Bay, with its numerous luxurious hotels, restaurants, and other recreational facilities, is Malta's topmost entertainment venue. It is somehow difficult to associate this zone with spectacular natural sites, folklore, and legend. And yet, just about 60 metres away from this bay, there lies a remarkable cavern that hides a subterranean world which only a few people have ever laid eyes on. This cavern was discovered a long time ago; however, since it is located on private land, access to it has always been limited.

In *Della Descrittione di Malta* (1647), Giovanni Francesco Abela refers to this cavern as 'Chark el Hamiem' but states that it was also known as 'Dragonara'. According to him, the former toponym related to a fissure in the cavern's ceiling from which one could access this place and through which pigeons flew to build their nests. He believed that the second toponym was associated with a local legend which narrated that a sea-monster lived within the darkness of this cavern. People swore that they could hear and feel the monster's chilling gurgles beneath their feet as they walked by. On rare occasions, they also saw it spraying water through the fissure. In his book *The Maltese Bestiary* (2014), Stephan D. Mifsud narrates this tale and provides an imaginary illustration of this monster.

The entrance shaft allows a beam of light to illuminate the bottom of the clear freshwater pool in an otherwise pitch-black cavern.

Going down the
stairs leading down
to the water.

He also draws attention to the curious fact that the nearby bay was named after St George who was renowned as a legendary dragon slayer.

Abela discarded all this as folkloristic myth and suggested that these sounds could have been caused by large eels which may have bred in the waters of the cavern. He explained the random splashes of water which came out of the cavern's roof to be the result of a sudden rush of the sea as it entered violently into the cave through subterranean channels.

Over the years, the name of this cavern has varied from Chark El Hamiem to Ħarq/Ħark Ħamiem/Ħammiem with *'chark/harq/hark'* meaning 'fissure', *hamiem* meaning 'pigeons', and *hammiem* being translated as a vessel for storing heat or a large vat for cooling water.

Caverna o abisso detto la dragonara scoperta in Malta a tre miglia dalla Città Valletta nel anno MDCXCV vicina a S. Guiliano abbattata da Casa Spinola.
Cristoforo de Lucia, pen-and-ink drawing of Ħarq Ħammiem and surrounding area.

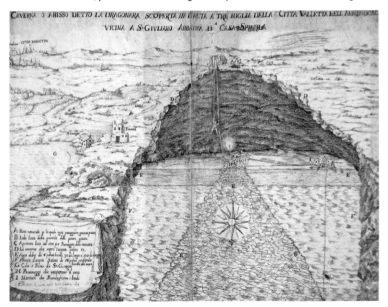

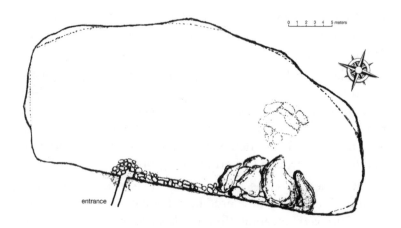

0 1 2 3 4 5 meters

entrance

Above: A plan of the cave. (courtesy: R. Borg-Bartolo and R. Aquilina, 1977)
Opposite: The dramatic height of the cave.

For many centuries, this cavern intrigued people to dare to explore its dark space and waters. One such survey was illustrated in a detailed cross-section drawing by Cristoforo de Lucia on 1 October 1695. Among the details shown, four men including a knight of the Order of St John are portrayed standing and sitting on a central high mound of stones which he claims to have been thrown there by passers-by through the opening. In the meantime, more men were lowered onto a raft to measure the water's depth.

In *Malta Illustrata* (1772) Count Giovan Antonio Ciantar says that another entrance was cut in the rock at the south side of the cavern in an attempt to turn it into an irrigation reservoir for Bailiff Spinola's residence which was located a short distance away. Apparently this idea was eventually abandoned but the narrow stepped passage is today the sole access to this enigmatic place.

In 1931, Sir Temi Zammit included this cavern in a booklet entitled *The Water Supply of the Maltese Islands* which covered

local hydrology. Later on, as various graffiti on the cavern walls close to the entrance indicate, during the Second World War, this site became quite well-known with the soldiers who were stationed at the military barracks nearby.

Further speleological research that took place in 1976 by a team that included Ramon Borg-Bartolo provided more information about this cavern. A plan published by Borg-Bartolo in *Heritage* (issue 14, p. 270) shows an elliptical cavern with an overall area of around 600 square metres at the water line. A fluctuation of 30 centimetres in the water-level was noticed between the dry and wet seasons. Moreover, the mean water-level was observed to roughly correspond to the sea water-level in St George's Bay.

The origins of this cavern are uncertain. During an interview for the TV documentary *Taħt l-Art*, John J. Borg, Senior Curator

The entrance to the cave.

An aerial view of St George's Bay showing (in red) the approximate reaches of the subterranean cave explored so far. The depths measured span all the way beneath the Institute of Tourism Studies (ITS) grounds.

at the National Museum of Natural History, said that it was formed through water erosion during the last Ice Age which happened around 10,000 years ago. It appears that at some point, the original cavern's heavy overhanging roof collapsed and created a sort of small island which is the only dry area in it. The presence of water in the cavern is due to rain water percolating through the rocks and sea-water seeping in from its depths.

From time to time, this cavern reveals another mystery about it and yet somehow it still continues to fool those who try to uncover all its secrets. During a survey commissioned by the government about 15 years ago, it was noted that the topmost point in the cavern was two storeys high, whereas the water's depth was 20 metres. However, although the divers thought that they would be exploring only the cavern's area, they were amazed to discover that it led to another underwater

The east (deep) side of the cave. From here the freshwater meets the sea and reaches depths still unknown. Notice the dangling roots penetrating the ceiling of the cave to reach the water.

opening. They also found a layer of sulphur at a depth of 12–15 metres and then more sea-water mixed with fresh water until they reached a depth of 52 metres below sea level. A further dive undertaken about 5 years ago to film footage for the afore-mentioned documentary confirmed that the end of this cavern could not be found since the divers were unable to proceed beyond the recorded depth as it was too dangerous to continue whilst carrying all their equipment.

Total darkness reigns in this monumental cavern throughout the entire day. Only artificial light will reveal the creepy thick roots which have penetrated through 11 metres of rock to reach down to the humid ambience and the clear fresh water. One can only wonder what this ancient cavern might have witnessed over the centuries and whether any life has ever lurked or still exists within its unknown depths.

Ħarq il-Ħammiem Cave has been scheduled at Grade 1 degree of protection by the Planning Authority. Hopefully the planned regeneration of Paceville which includes a proposed 5-star hotel, residences, commercial office space, a casino, a shopping mall, restaurants, and a basement car park on this site, will leave no negative impacts on this unique natural site.

8

CURIOUS TOWER HOUSES

Two Ħaż-Żabbar Dwellings

Some particular buildings have always stood out among the rest. Their exceptional design reflected the whimsical mind of their designer but often such structures were destined to become mere curiosities, especially when no one has any idea why they were built that way.

Two such buildings located in Ħaż-Żabbar are both used as residences; the only extraordinary thing about them is that

'Lourdes House' in Xgħajra Street, Ħaż-Żabbar.

Detail of one of the corner turrets on the Xgħajra side.

their upper floors resemble small towers. Intriguingly, these houses which are situated at a considerable distance from each other share common characteristics which indicate that the owners may have known each other and that probably the same architect was involved in their design. Curiously both houses are associated with Mary, the Mother of Jesus, and the two display marble slabs with religious indulgences.

One of the houses is situated in Xgħajra Street. Its parapet wall is heavily designed and shaped like a tower with a turret at each end of the façade. No one knows why this property was constructed in this way. Yet the oddness of this residence does not end there since a large niche was also assembled in the centre of the upper floor. Locals call this building 'Lourdes House' and they all insist that this niche was built in devotion to the Marian apparitions which were reported in Lourdes by Bernadette Soubirous in 1858. Indeed the niche replicates this apparition, cave and all. An inscription on the façade, dated 30 August 1897, promises 40 days of divine indulgence to those who recite a *Salve Regina* in front of the house. Interestingly, a painting in Ħaż-Żabbar Parish Hall depicts this house.

Researchers Karmenu Bonavia and Michael Buhagiar write that it was the Pace Spadaro family, well-known for its devotion towards Our Lady of Lourdes, who financed its construction. Is it just a coincidence that the road opposite the other house in Bajada Street is called Spadaro Street?

The niche in the façade replicates the Marian apparitions at Lourdes to Bernardette Soubirous in 1858.

The peculiar building known to the locals as 'The Madonna of the Military' in Bajada Street, Ħaż-Żabbar.

Although somewhat different, the second house bears the same tower formation on its parapet wall. However, this time, high up in the middle, there is a large turret with a statue of Our Lady on top with her child Jesus. People know this building as 'The Madonna of the Military' but nobody can explain why. Possibly this is because this title is mentioned in the inscription dated 20 September 1898 which is found on the marble slab attached to the façade. This time, the 40-day divine indulgence can be obtained by reciting an *Ave Maria* in front of the house.

Opposite: The peculiar building known to the locals as 'The Madonna of the Military' in Bajada Street, Ħaż-Żabbar. Below: The turret with the statue of Our Lady with her child Jesus.

9

FATAL ERRORS
The 1823 Carnival Tragedy, Valletta

Although Carnival is generally associated with fun and exuberance, the celebrations which took place on 11 February 1823 led to tragedy when over 100 children were killed in a stampede at the convent of the Franciscan Friars Minor (now known as *Ta' Ġieżu*) in Valletta. Ironically, the children were attending an activity that was meant to protect them from the typical diturbances and confusion which took place in the streets during Carnival.

Leading Maltese crime historian Edward Attard tells us how a report published in the *Malta Government Gazette* on Friday, 14 February 1823, describes in detail what happened on that fateful day. During the last days of Carnival, catechism teachers took a group of boys aged between 8 and 15 years who came from the lower classes of Valletta and the Three Cities to Floriana to hear mass. Then they took them back to the Valletta convent to be given some bread paid for by the government and other well-wishers.

As the police investigation stated, a succession of errors that ensued on that tragic day led to the fatal end. The first mistake was that the mass in Floriana lasted an hour longer than usual, thereby leading to the children's walk to Valletta coinciding

Opposite: Painting by Sir George Whitmore, witness to the 1823 Carnival tragedy, depicting a human stampede. (courtesy: Nicholas de Piro)

with the end of the Carnival celebrations when the crowds were returning home. The second blunder was when the vestry door that led to the convent's corridor was left open because the boys were late, giving the opportunity to other adults and children to steal in. The third error materialized when a lamp in the corridor suddenly went out, leaving everyone in darkness and panic ensued.

A door at the end of the corridor from where the children were to go out to receive the bread stood half-open so that no one would re-enter to take a second helping. This narrow exit on St Ursula Street became blocked when the boys and adults at the back of the dark corridor tried to rush out in panic, unknowingly crushing the ones at the front. Although people outside the convent rushed to assist the children when they heard their screams inside, by then 110 children had already died due to suffocation or as a result of being trampled upon.

Left: Ta' Ġieżu church. Right: The staircase in the corridor leading to the exit where the tragedy unfolded.

The door, and only exit,
giving onto St Ursola Street
that became a bottleneck
for the mass of children
trying to get out.

Not the Ku Klux Klan, but a member of the Archconfraternity of the Holy Rosary among whom were some of Malta's most prominent personalities.

10

TILL DEATH DO US PART

The Archconfraternity of the Holy Rosary, Valletta

Knowing that you're bound to be executed must be a terrible experience and waiting for it to happen must surely be a painful period of time, especially if you are alone. Although they could not interfere with the death penalty, members of the Archconfraternity of the Holy Rosary dedicated themselves to alleviating the terror and pain of prisoners condemned to death by standing beside them and offering them spiritual comfort during the last days of their lives.

Collecting alms for masses for the repose of the soul of a condemned criminal. *(Illustrated London News, 1882)*

The Archconfraternity members with habits blowing in the wind walking in procession through Merchants Street in Valletta, probably singing the *De Profundis*, immediately following an execution.

The Archconfraternity of the Holy Rosary was instituted in Valletta in 1575 by a group of knights of the Order of St John. Its members were mostly knights and prominent citizens who committed themselves to support prisoners and their families and to encourage the recitation of the Holy Rosary.

Once the members were notified by the prison authorities of an impending execution, each one would go around a particular town or village to collect money to support the prisoner's family and to celebrate masses for the repose of the soul of the condemned man. No money was collected from the place where the crime was committed or from the area where the prisoner's family resided.

People recognized the archconfraternity's members from their singular white habit which included a hat, gloves, a corded girdle with a hanging rosary, and a hood to keep their identity secret. Many tried to help as they could by dropping

Collecting alms for masses for the repose of the soul of a condemned criminal.

The Public Hanging outside Kordin Prison, 1860, watercolour by E.H. Thurlow. Notice the Archconfraternity member in the white habit and hat in the foreground. (courtesy: Albert Ganado)

Two surviving wooden *tavolette* belonging to the Archconfraternity of the Holy Rosary depicting a crucifixion scene (left) and the Virgin of the Rosary flanked by Saints Dominic and Joseph (right). A friar would climb a ladder and hold a *tavoletta* close to the face of the condemned at the point of execution. It was believed that this would see the convict to a peaceful death. (courtesy: Nicholas de Piro)

money in the collection tin that was carried along the streets by these hooded men in utter silence.

During the last three days prior to the execution, members of this guild would accompany the prisoner and even offer him the opportunity to join the archconfraternity. When it was time for the execution, the prisoner would be shown two wooden palettes with the images of Our Lady of the Holy Rosary and Our Lady of Sorrows imprinted on them respectively so that he could look at them with devotion and die a peaceful death. After the execution, the members would take care of the prisoner's corpse, paying the costs of the funeral and also seeing to his burial.

The death penalty in Malta was abolished in 1971, yet the last execution took place in 1943. Nevertheless the Archconfraternity of the Holy Rosary is still active to this day and its rector is the Marquis Nicholas de Piro.

The grim spectacle taking place at the top of Merchants Street following the execution of Giuseppe Pace in 1927. (courtesy: McCarthy's PhotoWorks)

M.C. Escher's *Balcony*, lithograph printed in 1945. (© 2017, The M.C. Escher Company – The Netherlands. All rights reserved. www.mcescher.com)

11

A GEOMETRIC SORCERY

M.C. Escher and Malta

The picturesque architecture of the historical harbour town of Senglea never fails to enchant visitors. It surely captivated the interest of one of the world's most famous graphic artists when he came over to Malta on a cargo ship in 1935. M.C. (Maurits Cornelis) Escher spent only a few hours there, just the time required to load and unload the ship's merchandise. Yet a detailed sketch he made that day served him to create two prints: *Balcony* and *Print Gallery,* which eventually became highly popular with his followers.

It took Escher ten years to publish the lithograph *Balcony* (1945). The harmonious and well-balanced structure of Senglea's background was ideal for the artistic expression that he had in mind. By warping one of the balconies into an imaginary circle, he expanded the centre of the scene and squeezed together its circumference, thereby creating a bizarre bulge-like appearance as though the picture were inflated from behind.

Ten years more elapsed and Senglea's scene was again a source of inspiration when Escher decided to try his hand at creating an annular bulge. This masterpiece, which became known as *Print Gallery* (1956), was formed by skilfully mounting a part of the original sketch onto a grid and twisting it into a geometric sorcery to create a fantastic illusion where there is no beginning and no end. In fact, the image shows a man looking at a print in an art gallery where the scene he is admiring is the same one in which he is standing.

In a letter to his son Arthur, he wrote about this lithograph: 'I don't think I have ever done anything as peculiar in my life. Among other things, it shows a young man looking with interest at a print on the wall of an exhibition that features himself. How can this be? Perhaps I am not far removed from Einstein's curved universe.'

Strangely, the artist decided to leave the centre of his masterpiece unfinished. The circular white patch in the middle of the lithograph, like virtually all of his other works, contains Escher's monogram, date of the print's completion and signature.

Photograph of Maurits Cornelis Escher, 1971.

M.C. Escher's *Print Gallery,* lithograph printed in 1956. (© 2017, The M.C. Escher Company – The Netherlands. All rights reserved. www.mcescher.com)

12

A VILLAGE RIGHT OUT OF THE MOVIES

Popeye Village, Mellieħa

An unusually colourful village completely built in wood awaits the curious visitor who approaches the area of Anchor Bay below Mellieħa. Crooked chimneys, warped slanted roofs looking like chocolate pieces, and ladders leading to nowhere are some of the bizarre things which can be noticed at Popeye Village. While today this site is an open-air museum and a family entertainment complex, in 1980 it served as the fictitious 'Sweethaven'; hometown to the whimsical cartoon character

Popeye the Sailor Man in the musical production *Popeye*, starring actor Robin Williams in his first big screen appearance.

'I had to negotiate with film director Robert Altman,' revealed Narcy Calamatta, who at the time was the managing director of Mediterranean Film Studios. 'I did a location hunt with the film designer in order to find an ideal spot where we could build the film set. I knew Anchor Bay well because it was just near my army camp.

'Paramount producer Bob Evans and his team came over and we signed a contract with the government to use the land to build the film set. Once we agreed about the location, I had to convince him that we could find wood in Malta.'

Since no wood resources were available on the island, everything had to be imported. Logs were brought from Holland and wood shingles came all the way from Canada. It took an international crew of 165 people to build an authentic

Robin Williams (Popeye) with Shelley Duvall (Olive Oyl), 1980. (Paramount Pictures)

Sweethaven, Malta's only pitched-roof village.

wooden village consisting of 20 structures. Works included also the construction of a 60-metre breakwater to protect the village from being battered by the sea.

'There was a clause in our contract which gave us the option to ask for the removal of this film set in order to render the place as it was originally or to leave the village there. I had a big fight with Robert Altman because he wanted me to pull it down. Yet I insisted that I was going to open it as a tourist attraction, which I did in 1982,' affirmed Calamatta.

Today this film set is open to the public all year round. It is one of the island's major tourist attractions and it is a must for those travelling with children. A fissure in a rock formation towering above Popeye Village's Anchor Bay has recently stirred much apprehension with many wondering if the rocks were in imminent risk of collapse, carrying the much-loved film set with it. These concerns swelled after the heartbreaking collapse of the Azure Window in Dwejra, Gozo, on 8 March 2017. Geologists, however, allayed fears stating that the fracture above Anchor Bay has existed for hundreds of years and does not threaten the picturesque site.

A rare photograph of the bay before the set was built showing a number of large anchors scattered on the sand. In 1907 a warehouse was built at Anchor Bay to be used for tuna-fishing purposes. These huge fishing nets were anchored to the seabed by means of heavy anchors and their presence here gave the bay its name. (source: Doris Fenech) The breakwater seen in the photograph is still *in situ.*

13

A SUNKEN TEMPLE

The Chapel of Bones, Valletta

Old guidebooks and travelogues are evident proof that Valletta's Chapel of Bones was extremely popular with both locals and tourists, at times even more than St John's co-cathedral. Its name stems from the fact that this underground vault was gruesomely decorated with human bones.

A few such eerie places can be found all around the world; at least two of them were in Malta. While the Capuchin crypt

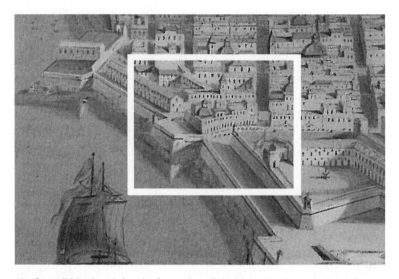

The first Nibbia church (marked) was demolished in 1730. The underground crypt, which was later to house the notorious bone display, survived this move. (image detail from Joseph Goupy, 1689–1769)

in Floriana is still extant, it is dubious whether the Chapel of Bones that was located close to Fort St Elmo, has been completely destroyed or not.

In 1612 Fra Giorgio Nibbia, a knight of St John, built a small church and crypt in the grounds of the cemetery that was situated close to the Sacra Infermeria (hospital), abutting the curved anatomical theatre. The church and its crypt actually stood where today's Evan's Building and carpark are sited, facing St Elmo and the granaries, and not where the present sign erroneously marks 'Chapel of Bones', just a few metres away.

This common misnomer arises from the fact that, as historian Giovanni Bonello has pointed out, this church was demolished in 1730 to make way for an extension of the women's hospital, known as the *Casetta*. The underground crypt, which was later to house the notorious bone display, survived this move. The second Nibbia church was erected in 1731, a stone's throw away from its predecessor, precisely where the present sign on North Street incorrectly reads 'Chapel of Bones'. The *Casetta* was later replaced by the Valletta elementary school in 1904; the Chapel of Bones remained intact.

The cemetery where the chapel stood was used to inter the patients who died in the hospital but, in 1776, when it reached its full capacity, its grounds were abandoned and left in neglect. To avoid the spread of disease, in 1845 the remaining human remains were gathered and deposited in the cemetery's crypt.

What happened next is still uncertain. Giovanni Bonello gives two versions. One of them states that, in 1847, Fr G. Zammit, the chaplain of the civil hospital, decided to decorate the crypt with human bones. Another theory says that, in 1895, a chaplain or verger from the nearby (second) Nibbia church

The second Nibbia church (left), erroneously referred to as the Chapel of Bones, was built in 1731 on the site facing the entrance to the Holy Infirmary on North Street. (courtesy: Palazzo Falson Historic House Museum)

Morbidly beautiful. In 1908, the entrance fee to the Chapel of Bones was of one penny. (courtesy: Anthony Abela Medici)

The devastation of the area between, and including, the second Nibbia church (left) and the Valletta Elementary School following the raids of 1941. The subterranean Chapel of Bones was buried somewhere to the right of this image and might have even survived the blast. (courtesy: Mark Vella NWMA)

Rows of skulls lining the walls of the chapel. (courtesy: Anthony Abela Medici)

removed the human remains from the hospital cemetery and used them to decorate the wall of the underground chapel.

In the early 1920s, the archbishop closed the chapel to visitors but it was reopened by the government in 1924. Entrance tickets were issued by the Department of Public Works. A postcard of this macabre site dating to 1908 indicates an entrance fee was of one penny.

Eventually this place was closed by Sir Temi Zammit, Director of the National Museum.

The Latin inscription on the main altar read:

The world is a theatre and human life is really a tragedy. Every earthly thing is a personification of vanity. Death breaks and dissolves the illusion and is the boundary of earthly things. Let those who visit this place ponder over these maxims. Pray for perpetual rest to the dead lying herein and carry with them a lively recollection of death – Peace be with you.

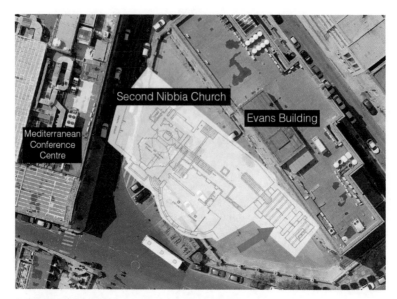

A 1915 Works Department plan of the Chapel of Bones area (courtesy: Giovanni Bonello) superimposed on the same site today, showing the actual location where the subterranean temple lies buried.

On the night of 14 February 1941, a German bombing raid demolished the elementary school (which stood close or over the Chapel of Bones) and severely damaged the second Nibbia church nearby.

It is widely believed that during this attack the Chapel of Bones was lost forever. However, other researchers such as architect Edward Said claim that, despite the damage on surface level, this chapel could possibly still exist beneath the parking area in front of Evans Building, waiting to be rediscovered. A plan of the former Chapel of Bones and adjacent edifices superimposed over today's site (see image above) places its whereabouts in the carpark area in front of Evans Building, somewhere between the second and seventh right-bay windows.

14

VALLETTA'S BEST-KNOWN SECRET
City Lights Adult Cinema, Valletta

For centuries, St John Street in Valletta acted as a link between the sacred and the profane. During the British Period, visitors could choose to visit the solemn splendour of St John's co-cathedral or move farther down the street to reach the red-light district in Strait Street. In later years, an adult movie theatre started to operate just a few metres away from the cathedral within a building which was originally used for ecclesiastical purposes.

There was nothing to indicate that soft porn or hard-core films were showing in this cinema. No adverts or posters were ever seen anywhere and yet this place was Valletta's best-known secret, especially with the locals. Unknowing people who happened to pass by at the right time would often be perplexed to hear sensuous sounds emanating from inside.

Although the movies shown were of a heterosexual nature, the cinema was a renowned hub for older men and homosexuals. Some of those who attended complained that the place was gloomy and dirty while others openly commented in online forums that the erotic services offered in the back rows were quite unique and thrilling and rarely encountered elsewhere.

Below: The staircase leading to the ticket booth. Opposite: St John Street and the Citylights Cinema.

The entrance fee of 5 euros entitled patrons to attend the cinema throughout the whole day, leaving and returning at will. A second entrance at the rear of the building led to Carts Street and it provided a convenient way to access the place without being seen.

A few years ago the owner, Alex Baldacchino, was prohibited from showing such films. Film critic Lino Cassar, who had also served as chairman of the censorship board in the past said: 'It had been open for at least 25 years. I cannot make heads or tails as to why the police had to intervene now when for so many years, the cinema was located just round the corner from the police station.' Lino Cassar explained that Baldacchino, would purchase reels from Sicily that would otherwise be disposed of, and then screen them at the City Lights without advertising them or showing the name of the film. Baldacchino asserted: 'whoever liked the genre knew that they could watch porn films at the City Lights, this was no secret.'

Yet the building's doorways, which lead also to a disused shopping complex, are often open for those curious enough to peep inside. Recently, the cavernous interior adjacent to the infamous theatre has been harmoniously converted to a cinema-themed bar making use of the original chairs and old film reels as decorations. No other adult movie theatres are available in Malta.

15

A HISTORICAL MUTILATION

A French Cannonball in the Wall, Ħaż-Żabbar

Initially, one might notice nothing extraordinary while moving out of Misraħ is-Sliem and passing through the short narrow stretch at the beginning of Bajada Street in Ħaż-Żabbar. Yet, a closer investigation of the upper façade of one of the old houses centrally situated on the left-hand side of this passage will reveal a historical cannonball embedded in the corner of the building.

The French artillery cannonball lodged in the façade of the Ħaż-Żabbar house.

Bajada Street, Ħaż-Żabbar. The house with the pockmarked façade is on the left.

The Maltese countryside rose in revolt against the French on 2 September 1798 and drove their overlords behind the city gates.

A plaque on the façade states that this cannonball has been lodged in this wall ever since the French attack on the village on 5 October 1798. At the time, the simmering discontent of the locals against the French occupiers had erupted into an insurrection and the French troops had been forced to withdraw behind the fortifications of Valletta, the Three Cities, and the harbours.

On this fateful day, hundreds of French soldiers rushed out of their positions through Notre Dame Gate (the central gate of the extensive Cottonera Lines facing Ħaż-Żabbar) to attack the nearby villages but the inhabitants were waiting for them. In the ensuing battle the French managed to reach the heart of Ħaż-Żabbar which was one of the bases of the Maltese

Notre Dame Gate on the Cottonera Lines from where the shot was probably fired.

insurgents. Many were wounded and killed that day but it was the French who suffered the heaviest losses.

Although some say that the French soldiers fired this cannonball during this assault, others are of the opinion that this incident might have taken place during other French attacks on this location. Indeed, further damage lower on the same elevation of the building's façade is said to have been caused by another cannonball which was also stuck in the wall but fell off recently.

16

A LONG LAYOVER

Super Constellation Bar and Snack Bar, Ħal Kirkop

A few fields away from Ħal Kirkop cemetery, there is a small area which is very popular for aircraft spotting. Ironically, though the landing aeroplanes attract much of these enthusiasts' attention, probably few ever notice the solitary plane engine which lies in this same corner and has an awesome story to tell.

Originally this engine belonged to a Super Constellation aircraft which was impounded in Malta in 1968 after it was discovered that it was carrying an illegal cargo. The aircraft

The plane by the roadside must have been quite a distraction. (courtesy: Gary Vincent)

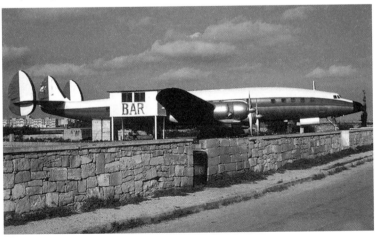

The Super Constellation Bar and Snack Bar. (courtesy: Michael Cassar)

was eventually released and sold at auction in 1973 and towed to a field near Ħal Luqa airport.

Later that year, the aircraft was sold again to an entrepreneur who had decided to turn it into a snack bar. However, this was not an easy task. The plane's wings had to be removed temporarily in order to transport it along the road to a field in Ħal Kirkop; then water and electricity services had to be provided.

Once open for the public, the Super Constellation Bar and Snack Bar made quite a hit with both locals and tourists, especially since the plane's cockpit and engines had been left intact. Those who visited it many years ago remember it as an outstanding if crammed venue. This business closed after 14 years of service and the aircraft found itself left to its destiny once again.

In 1997 the remnants of the plane which had been severely vandalized over the years were destroyed in a fire. Its engines, however, were salvaged and one of them was placed opposite the snack bar's original location.

A photo moment while driving past the unusual snack bar in Triq San Nikola, Ħal Kirkop.

Left: The bar's own passbook – a loyalty card masked as a passport. (photo by Peter Beetschen) Right: Super Constellation Snack Bar souvenir matchboxes. (photos by Clive Samudi)

17

BURIED ALIVE

Wied Għammieq Cemetery, Kalkara

Far away from the crowds, at Rinella in Kalkara, there is Wied Għammieq cemetery which was built to receive the corpses of those who died during the cholera epidemic of 1837. Yet old rumours persist in alleging that not only the dead were buried there.

The first cases of this cholera epidemic were identified at the Ospizio, which was a hospital for old people in Floriana. As a safety measure to isolate this outbreak, it was decided to move the troops from Fort Ricasoli in Kalkara in order to transfer the whole hospital establishment together with the patients there. However, this decision was changed when more patients died while those who had not yet shown any symptoms and had relatives and friends ready to take care of them, were allowed to leave. At the time, the authorities believed that cholera was not a contagious disease. They were soon proved wrong when cholera started to spread like wildfire across Malta.

As the number of cholera victims kept increasing and it was realized that this disease was terribly contagious, people were terrified to touch, let alone bury the dead. It is said that Sicilian prisoners were brought over to Malta to do this horrible job, being promised to be released if they survived the ordeal.

So many people died that local cemeteries started to reach saturation point and new burial sites had to be found. These

Wied Għammieq cemetery just outside Fort Ricasoli, Kalkara with the monument erected in memory of the victims of the cholera epidemic of 1837.

included the cemetery in Wied Għammieq which was built near Fort Ricasoli. Death was all over the place and the numerous corpses had to be dealt with immediately. Rumours say that in the frenzy to remove the victims as quickly as possible from the rest of the population, there were occasions when people were buried alive by mistake. This gruesome situation was recognized when individuals who happened to pass hurriedly by the area heard desperate cries coming from beneath the tombstones.

In 1881 the remains of all the corpses in this cemetery were exhumed and placed together in an ossuary. A monument was also erected in their memory. From then on, a traditional annual pilgrimage started to take place to this cemetery with people from various parishes gathering to hear mass and pray for the souls of these unfortunate victims. This pilgrimage still takes place each year at the beginning of November.

Wied Għammieq cemetery gate.

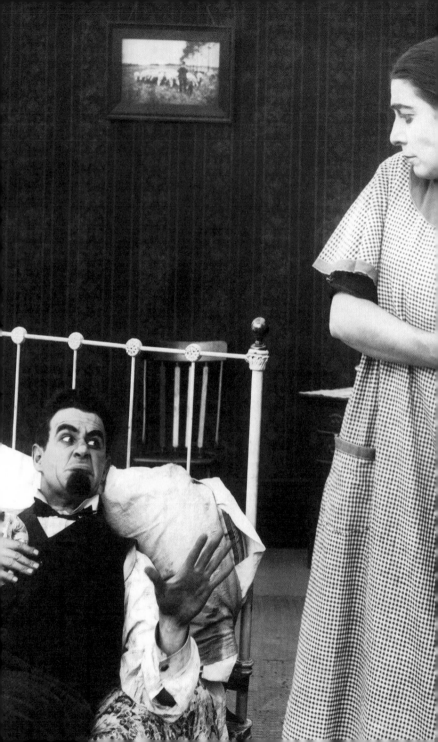

18

AS THE WIND BLOWS
Xatrambatra

Sciatara-e-matara is a Sicilian expression which can be translated as 'Oh good God!' and shows preoccupation at something which has taken place or is about to happen. Who knows whether this has anything to do with the old Maltese word *xatrambatra* which was a device that served to prevent the stink of breaking wind in bed?

Apparently the *xatrambatra* was made from a dried long gourd which was hollowed out and attached to a pipe. One would tie this piece of equipment to one's buttocks just before getting into bed and then direct the attached pipe outside the bed-covers before lying down to sleep. This precaution was intended to avoid the embarrassment of breaking wind while in bed with one's partner and entrapping the pong under the sheets.

It is believed that the *xatrambatra* was mainly used by newly married couples, particularly those from noble families. Made of copper, silver, and sometimes gold, depending on the status of the person, this contraption formed part of the bride's dowry during the nineteenth century.

19

INCONGRUENT CONCRETE
World War II Relics on the Shoreline, Marsaskala

The St Thomas Bay area in Marsaskala is an idyllic, perhaps little appreciated, spot where one can relish a swim in the crystalline sea or enjoy a relaxing walk in the countryside. Yet in the past, this bay was far from welcoming and proof of this is provided by three large concrete blocks, triangular in shape with rusting metal hooks at the top that are completely alien to their surroundings.

Opposite: One of the three concrete blocks that can be seen on the beach.
Below: Aerial view of St Thomas Bay.

During the rule of the Order of St John, the location was well known to pirates, owing to its easy accessibility. They often raided nearby villages whenever they succeeded to land without being noticed. In the eighteenth century, Riħama Battery was constructed to defend this area. It even opened fire on the French invaders, but it soon fell to the enemy. Later the building served as a soap factory, then as a slaughterhouse, and finally as a farm.

During the Second World War, the fear of another invasion in this area led the authorities to place obstacles on the shore of the bay. Known as dragon's teeth, these pyramidal masses were designed to impede the movement of enemy landing craft and vehicles. They were made of concrete and had a triangular shape, with heavy angle-iron spikes jutting out of each slanting face. They were removed after the war, except for three which were left in the area. Very few people are aware that these crumbling and rusty strange objects are historical military artefacts. Indeed, it is not unusual to see rubbish bags waiting for collection attached to their hooks.

The top hooks aptly look like question marks whereas the iron spikes have been hacked for safety reasons (photo: Fiona Vella).

20

A GROTESQUE CELEBRATION

Nadur's Spontaneous Carnival, Gozo

Around 4,000 people live in Nadur in Gozo, making it one of the largest villages on the island. However, during the Carnival season, it attracts over 30,000 visitors. The allure lies in the spontaneous activities that take place and in the grotesque masked figures which roam its streets at night during this festive period. Held for many years as Nadur's best-kept secret, these creepy celebrations have become quite renowned and are now considered as one of the ten most bizarre Carnivals around the world.

The dark festivities take place during the four days preceding Ash Wednesday or the beginning of Lent. The first strange characters appear as soon as the sun sets but eerie creatures continue to crop up until very late at night. Originally, the game was mainly about disguise and participants did their utmost not to be recognized. They wore unusual costumes and hid their faces behind masks and hoods while keeping silent in order to remain anonymous. Carnival floats were made out of discarded material that was creatively turned into various weird means of transport.

Although the central theme of this Carnival remains macabre, contemporary revellers have introduced several other features which enhance the chaotic nature of these improvised celebrations. The number of food and drink vendors has

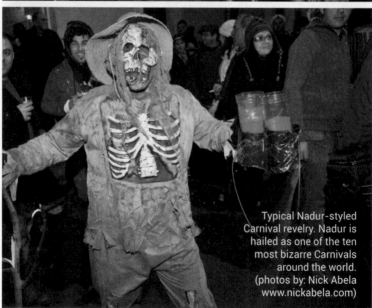

Typical Nadur-styled Carnival revelry. Nadur is hailed as one of the ten most bizarre Carnivals around the world. (photos by: Nick Abela www.nickabela.com)

Typical Nadur Carnival scenes. (courtesy: Nick Abela – www.nickabela.com)

increased considerably, whilst the participation of rock bands have added to the anarchic fun.

In spite that everything is done in the name of entertainment, in 2009 several participants in this Carnival ended up in court after dressing up as Jesus Christ and nuns. The bishops of Malta and Gozo both condemned these acts which they deemed offensive to the Catholic religion. Eventually the man who dressed up as Jesus was given a one-month jail term suspended for 18 months, whereas the six who dressed as nuns were acquitted. Up to a few years ago, Maltese law did not allow people to wear ecclesiastical habits or vestments without an adequate permit and gestures and words which might vilify religion were strictly prohibited. Not everyone agreed with this decision and the following year, a Facebook group was set up to encourage people to dress up as Jesus as a form of protest. Police presence was increased to ensure that public morals are respected and they demanded to vet the rock bands' songs in an attempt to eradicate offensive or vulgar lyrics. Yet the latter decision was reconsidered after it created a hot controversy. Malta has since revised its vilification laws, with Minister for Justice Owen Bonnici saying that 'in a democratic country, people should be free to make fun of religions, while not inciting hatred.'

Carnival festivities are deeply ingrained in Maltese culture and any efforts to impose bans on it have always proved futile. One of the most renowned such incidents goes back to the seventeenth century when Grand Master Jean-Paul de Lascaris-Castellar issued an order which prohibited women from wearing masks and costumes that represented the devil and from participating in the knights' banquets. This resolution caused so much ferment that it was soon abolished. To this day, a popular Maltese saying which is used to describe a very bitter person goes: '*Qisek wiċċ Laskri*' which literally translates to 'You look like Lascaris'.

Grand Master Lascaris,
forever immortalized in
Maltese cultural memory as
the ultimate party pooper.

21

A PECULIAR GROOVED SEABED
Marsaskala's Underwater Lines

Munxar near Marsaskala is indeed a spectacular place. Open fields bloom with various coloured wild flowers and shrubs according to season, while the blue-green sea blends charmingly with the white chalky cliffs. Caves, layered strata, and other geographical features can be admired in the area and one can't help wonder how ancient this view really is.

A tantalizing aspect in this idyllic scene is the bizarrely grooved seabed which can be clearly seen from the cliffs above. Some insist that these numerous canals, a number of which

appear to be parallel, are part of the famous and mysterious cart-rut systems that can be found around the islands. Others, however, maintain that they are just the result of common natural erosion in the seabed.

Bird's-eye-view of the bizarrely-grooved seabed.

22

AN UNIDENTIFIED MONUMENT

The Three Crosses at Il-Bidni, Marsaskala

The Monument of the Three Crosses stands secluded in the Bidni area, right opposite the old church dedicated to Our Lady of Light, in the limits of Ħaż-Żabbar. It consists of three stone crosses standing on pedestals with the central one bearing detailed passion symbols. Mystery surrounds this religious structure since it is not known who erected this monument and for what reason.

Insets of the passion symbols on the central cross.

One theory says that it was set up to indicate the limits of Żejtun and Ħaż-Żabbar. However, author Ġużè Muscat Azzopardi provides us with three other traditional versions. The first one states that this site marks a grave of three monks who were killed by the Turks. The second says that this spot was used by the people of Żejtun to bury a man who died of plague. The third hypothesis is the weirdest of them all: it claims that an elderly hermit was inhumed here, after he repeatedly rose three times from the dead.

23

AN EERIE DISCOVERY
The 1813 Plague Cart, Ħaż-Żabbar

The Sanctuary of Our Lady of Graces at Ħaż-Żabbar attracts many visitors both due to its architectural splendour and also because of the miraculous reputation of the village's patron saint. Numerous ex-voto have been donated to this church which, together with various other interesting items, can be admired at the Żabbar Sanctuary Museum located adjacent to it.

The horrors of the 1813 plague. A hearse can be seen on the right while, at top right, a man shoots a cat as these were thought to spread the contagion.

Forzati. Convicted criminals were forced into service to carry and bury corpses and to clear infected houses. Their faces covered and working under surveillance, they were promised freedom if they survived the epidemic. Most of them died. (sketch by Sir George Whitmore)

Ex-voto painting at Our Lady of Mellieħa Sanctuary showing plague barriers outside City Gate and the infamous death hearse being towed outside Valletta.

Drawing by Sir George Whitmore showing doctors testing the scabs of a plague victim from a safe distance during the 1813 epidemic.

One of the most curious exhibits in this museum is a portable wooden coffin which was used during the plague of 1813. Since all such items connected with the outbreak were burnt in order to put an end to this contagious disease, it is a mystery how this object has avoided destruction.

Many valuable things were lost during the frightful periods whenever the islands were hit by epidemics of plague. Paper was believed to be one of the culprits in spreading the disease and there were instances when several books and whole archives which belonged to plague victims were destroyed.

Not much was known about these epidemics, whether they were contagious or not and how they were transmitted from one person to another. Indeed, for a time, wood was used instead of paper since it was not known that even this material could carry this deadly disease. Contracts written on pieces of wood bear witness to this misunderstanding. Once wood was identified as a possible carrier, anything made from this material that came into contact with a plague victim

Frans Gafà with the plague cart discovered in the crypt of the Ħaż-Żabbar sanctuary. (photo: Fiona Vella)

was immediately burnt. Therefore the recent discovery of a cart which is believed to have carried such corpses is quite astonishing.

As Frans Gafà was doing some work in the sanctuary's charnel house, he came across a strange object buried in the soil. He called out to others to help him pull it out and, when he opened its lid, he noticed that there was some black writing scribbled across it on the inside which read: '*Questa cascia fatta il 10 Luglio 1813, la Sinor Maestro Gioachino Xerri per carreggiare li pestiferi morti*' (This cart was made on 10 July 1813, Mr Gioachino Xerri to carry the infected deceased). The lid was taken to a priest who was horrified when he deciphered the writing.

Immediate action was taken to verify that none of the people involved in this find had exposed themselves to the disease. After it was restored, this unique cart became one of the main exhibits in this museum.

24

HE PICKED SEASHELLS ON THE SEASHORE

The Seashells House in Ħal Għaxaq

Just a few metres away from the rear of Ħal Għaxaq's parish church, in St Mary Street, one cannot help noticing a very odd house named *Id-Dar tal-Bebbux* (literally translated as The House of the Snails) which is decorated with hundreds of seashells. These ornaments date back to 1898 when Indrì Dimech, known as *Il-Mikk*, decided to embellish the façade of his house with seashells that he collected from local and foreign beaches.

No one can really say what inspired Indrì to embark on such a project. Since he often worked as a sailor in the Middle East, some people suggest that he might have come across such decorations abroad. Some distant relatives of Indrì narrate that, whenever he was in Malta between 1898 and 1901, he would set up bedsheets to cover the façade of his house to continue working on his masterpiece. It is not known whether he did this to protect himself from the sun or whether he wanted to surprise his neighbours with his work.

More than a century later, Indrì's intricate seashell designs have somehow survived the tides of time. Many of the patterns bear a religious element and include angels, crosses, a church, and symbols connected with the Passion of Christ. Others show lions, unicorns, palm trees, a fountain, Ħal Għaxaq's coat of arms, and also his surname, Dimech.

The beauty of Indrì's work was further enriched with small stone statues and niches. A statue of Our Lady, the patron saint of Ħal Għaxaq, stands triumphantly on a large sphere of clouds high up on the main façade. One niche was dedicated to St Joseph, a very cherished saint in the village, another to St Andrew (Indrì in Maltese), while the third one shows a crucified Christ flanked by the Virgin Mary and St John the Evangelist.

The creator of the seashells house, Indrì Dimech, known as *Il-Mikk*. (courtesy: Darren Abela)

Today the property is a private residence but, in Indrì's time, it served as a

Despite its fame and it being an important landmark in dire need of conservation, the 'seashells house' is still not a listed building. (courtesy: Roderick Vella & Stephen Buhagiar – *The People of Malta*)

The façade of the house, corner with St Mary Street, with the statue of St Joseph in the small *pjazza*.

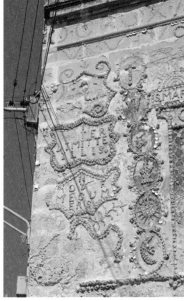

The frontispiece with the statue of Our Lady and the inscription '1901'.

bar wherein men gathered to have a drink and to socialize after a hard day's work. The place was also an attractive hub to those who were devoted and passionate about the feast of the Assumption of Our Lady; from there was born the idea of establishing the first social club in Ħal Għaxaq that was dedicated to the Assumption.

Even though Indrì's creation still manages to captivate the curiosity of passers-by, much of the seashell decorations are now in a very bad condition and are in dire need of restoration. A good number of seashells have already eroded away and are lost. Hopefully, this bizarre and unique structure will be saved in time to continue to amaze those who walk past it.

25

ABOVE THE CURVE

Magħtab's 'Acoustic Mirror', Naxxar

Looking across the countryside from the high ridge situated at the end of St Paul Street in the limits of Naxxar, just near the roundabout before going downhill to Salina Road (locally known as T'Alla u Ommu), one can enjoy a spectacular view of the northern side of Malta. Yet a very interesting feature lies in the plain below, to the right of the winding descent; it is a primitive enemy airplane detection structure.

The 'listening ear' was sheltered from background noise at its rear by the natural escarpment known as the Great Fault.

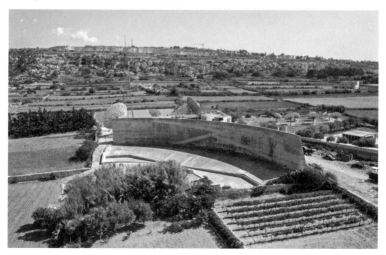

The incongruous structure in Tarġa Road referred to as a 'listening ear' by the British is known as *Il-Widna*, 'the ear'. The site was selected in 1933 after a thorough investigation of the island identified it as an adequate area for the construction of an acoustic mirror, since it is about two kilometres inland, faces out to sea towards Sicily, and is sheltered from other noise by the ridge at the its rear.

Acoustic mirrors originated in Britain towards the end of the 1920s as an early warning system to detect approaching enemy aircraft. They consisted of large reinforced concrete structures which could pick up noise from aircraft engines while they were still a considerable distance away.

Several acoustic mirrors were built in Britain and a number of others were planned to be set up in the primary British colonies of Malta, Gibraltar, and Singapore. Yet it was soon realized that these military structures had a major flaw as they picked up all the surrounding noises and it was impossible to discriminate between aircraft sound and any other noise.

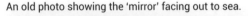

An old photo showing the 'mirror' facing out to sea.

A close-up view of the concave concrete wall.

In fact, no such structures were constructed in Gibraltar and Singapore. Although five locations were initially earmarked in Malta, the others being Marsaskala, Ħal Għaxaq, Mtaħleb, and Ħad-Dingli, only the one at Magħtab was built.

Its construction began in 1934 and it was ready a year later. Its design was very close to the acoustic mirror which is located at Denge, near Dungeness in Kent. From tests that were carried out, it was estimated that Malta's 'listening ear' was able to provide a six-minute warning of approaching aircraft at 250 mph. This provided enough time to prepare the anti-aircraft batteries and to warn civilians of an impending air raid.

Although it was still in an experimental phase, this structure was useful, especially at the brink of a Second World War. However, the development of faster aircraft in just a few years quickly turned these systems obsolete. *Il-Widna* was reported to be out of use by 5 May 1937 as a more advanced electronic system known as Radio Detection And Ranging (RADAR) was established. The Malta system was the first and only one tested outside the UK.

Aerial view showing the curvature of the wall.

The concrete parabolic structure measures 61 metres from end to end and rises to a height of 8.2 metres. The area is now used as an earth station by telecommunications company GO and there is therefore no direct access to the acoustic mirror. Nonetheless, visitors can get quite close to have a peek at it.

26

A MARQUIS' ARCHITECTURAL FOLLY

Villa Mystique, Madliena

It is difficult not to be captivated by the strange huge structure of a somewhat Gothic style which lies in Pedidalwett Street in Madliena. Even the most untrained eye would deem the building's design odd and outlandish. From its conception, Villa Mystique was intended to shock and amaze and, despite its present state of abandonment, its allure is still great if not greater.

Villa Mystique, Madliena – constructed from the debris of old Maltese houses bombed during World War II.

In his article 'Villa Mystique: An endangered folly', local architect Prof. Conrad Thake believes this building to be the only authentic architectural folly in Malta. Back in the early 1980s, as a young architectural student, he had the privilege to meet the man who gave it life: Marquis Joseph Scicluna (1925–95). He recalls being bewildered to learn that the marquis had no predetermined design for the villa and that he was constructing it according to his intuition, from time to time giving ad hoc instructions to his masons.

Probably, 'God's own eccentric', as author John Micallef referred to the marquis in his book *The Scicluna Saga 1772–2008* (2008), was only trying to impress and awe the students since a plan seems to have existed after all. This plan shows a completed Mystique with two connected towers; the space between the towers is developed and a roof restaurant is

Villa Mystique represents the triumph of free human spirit unshackled by institutional conformity and societal order.—Conrad Thake

Within today's building environment, Villa Mystique seems to chide us for the soulless, nondescript buildings we are producing. —Conrad Thake

envisaged. For some reason or another, this project was never concluded.

Marquis Joseph Scicluna, Baron of Tabria, was the son of the well-known philanthropist Marquis John Scicluna (1903–70), popularly known as *Iċ-Ċisk*. Although his family's strength lay in the finance business, Joseph was more attracted to music and art and was generally known as a free spirit. Whereas the Scicluna family owned some of the grandest properties in Malta, such as Palazzo Parisio in Naxxar and Balluta Buildings in St Julian's, the 4th Marquis opted to build his own masterpiece in the shape of Villa Mystique.

In a rare filmed interview by TVM/ABC (Australia), the marquis talks about himself and his creation. He insists that Mystique is entirely his own architecture, a product of his surrealistic imagination. He describes how he had constructed his villa from the debris of old Maltese houses bombed during

Conrad Thake vividly recalls the marquis addressing a group of architectural students, including himself, on a personal tour of Villa Mystique in 1983. The marquis was proud of the fact that he had no architect or pre-conceived plans to guide him and that he would give instructions on impulse to his two masons on the spot.

World War II, choosing interesting pieces and objects to give form to the fanciful ideas of his mind.

Some of those who had the opportunity to visit Villa Mystique often compared it to Gaudi's Park Guell in Barcelona. Maybe this is because the marquis opted to decorate his building with coloured glass and stones of various sizes. However, the resemblance ends there because the property, which enjoys breathtaking views of Wied Mejxu, is simply unique.

'Like the proverbial phoenix, I gathered all these bits and memories and I formed them into a sculpture,' declared the marquis. Indeed, the building is impregnated with parts of Maltese history and its soaring towers seem aimed to defy the enemy which had demolished the original houses by mounting the ruins right up to the sky in a grand style. The brightly coloured glass placed randomly in every nook and corner of the building sheds light and charm on materials

Like the proverbial phoenix, I gathered all these bits and memories and I formed them into a sculpture. —Marquis Joseph Scicluna

Top: The Gaudiesque undulating course at roof level with blue-and-turquoise-hued glass glistening in the sun. Below, left: A glass mosaic spells 'Mystic' on the eponymous tower. Below, right: The peacock mosaic on the upper terraces of the Mystic tower facing Wied Mejxu.

The crowning steeples of the Mystique tower seem to be vaguely inspired by Gaudi's architectural creations.

where darkness was supposed to reign, gloriously challenging the amazing natural hues of the surrounding environment.

Stones of every type and shape were used for the construction of the villa which was laid out in an organic design and split into two towers, 'Mystique' and 'Mystic', each with its own character but decorated in similar peculiar ways. Glass, marble, and stone pieces were embedded in the floors, walls, and ceilings, often arranged in bird, snake, or Maltese Cross designs, but also laid out haphazardly with no uniformity whatsoever. Rows of glass bottles were inserted in the walls to form bizarre mosaics while others were left on top of singular structures. Attractive stone ornaments, even broken ones, were integrated in the project.

Coats of arms with the motto *Robur Genialitatis Praemium* (Strength is the price for joviality) which adorn various parts of the building emphasize the philosophy of this eccentric marquis.

The cock – a common motif found throughout the edifice.

Above: The sun, moon, and star mosaics bask under the Madliena sky. Below, left: Tile-and-glass mosaic depicting a bird and a serpent. Below, right: The sun mosaic on the Mystique tower rooftop with Torri Pawlina in the background.

The staircase leading from the central courtyard to the upper levels of the Mystique tower.

Above, left: Pseudo-Gothic motifs on the upper terrace give it the sense of a majestic ruin. Above, right: The coat of arms with the motto 'Robur Genialitatis Praemium' (Strength is the price for joviality) can be seen in various parts of the complex. Below: A kaleidoscope of hues emanates from the broken polychromatic glass that bedeck the walls.

A bird's-eye view over the tower.

A panoramic view of the ground-floor level of the Mystique tower showing a bathtub reached by four steps and with an oculus directly overhead.

Top, left: Fanciful sculpture presents itself through the dense foliage. Top, right: A whimsical pointed archway in the heart of the complex. Above: *Marquis Joseph Scicluna* by Debbie Caruana Dingli.

Above: Villa Mystique from Tal-Ibraġ. Below, left: A circular aperture lined with pieces of glass looks onto the central courtyard. Below, right: A sculptural piece bathes in the sunlight in the lower courtyard.

Aerial view showing the sinuous forms that form and connect the two towers.

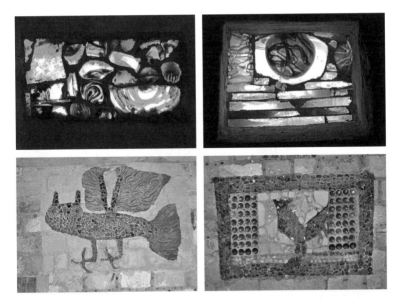

The brightly coloured glass placed at random in every nook and corner of the building sheds light and charm where darkness was supposed to reign.

Conrad Thake recalls the marquis telling university students about the time when a foreign architect, upon visiting Villa Mystique, shook his head and remarked: 'You have broken every bloody rule in architecture but, somehow, the end product is a thing of beauty.'

In its heyday, the property was even acclaimed internationally as a place of wonders. In the 1960s, Villa Mystique was turned into a sort of nightclub for people to meet, play music, and chill out. Later on, it was also briefly reopened as a restaurant.

The festive nature of Villa Mystique was terminated when the 4th Marquis passed away in Rome on 6 June 1995.

'When I die, I'd like to be buried in Mystique, not in a cemetery. We have our own private chapel in the cemetery, but I'd rather be buried where I built because that's part of me,' Marquis Joseph Scicluna had revealed in the afore-mentioned interview. Still his wish was not granted as on 14 June 1995, he was buried in the Scicluna family's private chapel in the West Section O-B-1 of the Addolorata Cemetery.

None of the magic has left the uncompleted building which seems to be waiting in suspense for the marquis' return to finish what he had begun. Several leading architects have urged for the preservation of this outstanding structure but so far Villa Mystique has not been granted the status of a protected building.

Opposite: *Mystique*, oil on board painting by Marquis Joseph Scicluna (1925–95).

British Royal Navy tradition promised quick promotion to junior officers who wriggled through the hook. From *The Daily Telegraph*, 1972. (courtesy: Michael Cassar)

27

A CONFOUNDING PROTRUSION

The Hook in St John Street, Valletta

A few metres away from St John's co-cathedral, at the corner of St John Street with Merchants Street, there is a strange large metal hook protruding from a wall just a few feet from the level of the street. Its original function is still a mystery and many tales have been associated with it. Some claim that this hook was used to hoist a large bell onto the steeple of the nearby St John's co-cathedral in the eighteenth century but this is just a myth.

The infamous hook in St John Street.

Another, more plausible, version which dates to the same period of the Order of St John's rule suggests that this hook was utilized to hold the ropes which hoisted convicted offenders above a column-like structure, or pillory, situated at the top corner of St John Street in order to expose them to punishment in public. Added to the humiliation, the gathering crowds would often jeer, mock and pelt the criminal with mud and rotten food. These prisoners were carried out from the Castellania, the eighteenth-century Baroque edifice in Valletta which served as a courthouse and prison. The hook is in fact lodged in the wall of this building in between the entrance to the cells and the pillory itself. Another use for the pillory was the gibbet which took the form of a metal cage used for the public display of the criminal's corpse after execution. Gibbeting remained in use in Malta well into the British era but, most probably, less here in the heart of city.

The Castellania building in Merchants Street.

Left: The corner of the Castellania, or law courts, between Merchants Street and St John Street where the pillar on which criminals were exposed to public ridicule still stands. Right: The opening atop the pillory from where the beam projected.

Various sources also point to the possibility of the hook being used in administering a form of torture known as the *strappado*. This consisted of a rope passed over a pulley, beam, or a hook, then tying the victims' arms behind their back and suspending them from the wrist. This caused intense pain as the internally-rotated shoulder sockets were often dislocated. At the corner of the building, high atop the pillory, an opening is still visible from where the beam once projected.

The legend of the hook persisted in later years and it became quite popular with British officers because of its rumoured connections with Lord Nelson. It is said that when Lord Nelson was in Malta in June 1803, after attending a dinner party in Valletta, he happened to walk down St John Street on his way back to his ship. When his officers saw the hook, they challenged him to wriggle himself through it and that's what he did! From then on, this piece of metal became renowned as Nelson's hook and junior officers who came to Malta were told to follow this vice-admiral's example if they wanted to gain promotion.

Some say that this tradition was still taking place up to the late 1950s, when there was still a substantial Royal Naval presence on the island. Locals remember many young officials being lured to this area on their way to 'The Gut', (as Strait Street, and its worldly pleasures, was known beyond these shores), and being taunted to go through the hook at which point they would be tied up to it and left there! Local historian Michael Cassar tells us that in 1899, for some obscure reason, the hook was removed only to be reinstalled sometime later following public outcry. To this day, locals refer to this part of St John Street as '*In-Niżla tal-Ganċ*' (the hill of the hook).

Detail from an early seventeenth-century painting of Valletta showing the first Castellania (long before it was redesigned to the building we see today) with the familiar rope and pulley mechanism used for gibbeting or torture already in place.

28

MALTA'S GHOSTLY RED-LIGHT DISTRICT
Strait Street, Valletta

Strait Street forms part of the gridiron network of Valletta's roads. It runs from St John Cavalier on Ordnance Street down to St Elmo Bay where it meets Fountain Street. Its name is descriptive of its narrow nature which becomes even narrower midway as it crosses Christopher Street behind St Catherine's monastery and descends steadily eastwards to within sight of Fort St Elmo.

Right from its construction in the sixteenth century, during the rule of the Order of St John and up to the final withdrawal of the British forces from Malta in 1979, this zone was a famous spot for taverns, music halls, and prostitution.

In his book *A Tour Through Sicily and Malta* (1773), the Scottish author Patrick Brydone states that in Hospitaller Malta, duelling was restricted only to Strait Street. He adds that a cross was always etched where a knight had been killed in a duel and that he had counted 20 of these crosses himself. Brydone may not be the most reliable of sources but there may be some truth to this tale.

In his enormously enjoyable article entitled 'The Voice of Valletta's Streets', Giovanni Bonello has this to say about the notorious street:

Legend wants Strait Street to have been deliberately built so narrow, for the purpose of duelling. The statutes of the Order punished this unolympic sport with expulsion when the combat was premeditated, but looked more leniently on it, if swords flashed in a sudden brawl. So, it is said, rivals staged their encounter in Strait Street, blaming it on some accidental collision in the constricted road. I have never come across any primary evidence to prove this deliberate piece of town-planning, though various duels were actually fought there.

During the British period, Strait Street lost its reputation as the arena for human blood sports, but achieved stardom for other amenities. It kept the brewers and the V.D. clinics in flourishing business.

Legend wants Strait Street to have been deliberately built so narrow for the purpose of duelling.—Giovanni Bonello. An artistic impression of a duel in the narrow street with crosses on the walls.

One of the attractions in Strait Street as recalled by servicemen on the walls of the Main Guard, Valletta. (courtesy: Michael Cassar)

When Malta became a British colony, Valletta, 'a city of palaces built by gentlemen for gentlemen' (Benjamin Disraeli, 1830), faced the reality of becoming the naval port of the Mediterranean Fleet with all the needs and demands that a naval garrison would expect to be satisfied. Author Eric Saxon in the British magazine *Titbits* (1965) describes Strait Street as an *'area of vice and prostitution that ranks with the world's most notorious sin-spots... a jungle of tiny bars and bedrooms where anything from striptease to demonstrations of the most revolting perversions can be arranged.'*

Though these observations would not surprise the modern reader, one has to imagine the sharp contrast of the worldly pleasures going on under the authorities' noses in a staunchly Catholic Malta at a time when even the circulation of the *Titbits* issue was banned.

When the British forces left Malta, the bars, restaurants, and entertainment places closed down one by one. Once alive with laughter, music, clinking bottles, bar brawls, and fist fights, this street fell silent, forlorn, and neglected. For a number of years, only the fading names of the empty shops hanging on to the crumbling façades remained to remind us of this area's history. The abandoned street, with its narrow and dark character was remembered only as a zone with connections to prostitution, and people avoided walking through it or hurried their pace if they had to pass through there. Locals who used to live or work in 'The Gut' refused to talk about their past experiences since they feared the consequences of being associated with its negative connotations.

Many young inexperienced sailors set themselves the Herculean task of imbibing one glass of alcoholic beverage from each bar situated in Strait Street. There were many bars and many contestants, but I neither know nor have heard of a single sailor completing this task.—Comment taken from an online Royal Navy forum.

*Strait Street was the matelots' centre
of the world above the equator.* —
Comment taken from an online
Royal Navy forum.
(courtesy: Bob Young & Joseph Borda)

Drunken sailors totter about in Strait Street. (drawing by Paolo Consiglio from *Colore di Malta* by Umberto Biscottini, 1941)

'The Gut', an apt name as just about everything flowed through there. It really came to life at night, all singing, all dancing, exciting, forbidden, dangerous, definitely not a place you could take your mother.—John Wiseman, Royal Malta Police. (courtesy: Derek Kelly & Jim Bryce)

89, Strait Street. Once a clinic for venereal disease is now home to a legal firm.

The Egyptian Queen, fondly remembered by all Navy men, stood on the corner of Old Theatre Street and Strait Street. (photo: *Life Magazine*)

Nevertheless, things changed considerably in these last few years when this taboo was shattered and 'The Gut' began to be appreciated for what it really was: a hub of entertainment where colourful and brightly-lit bars, music halls, lodging houses, and hotels lined the street and people from different nations cheered and sang together until they were dragged to their ships by the military police or the naval patrol.

Researchers focused their attention on this distinct zone, eager not to lose the collective memory related to 'The Gut'. Nowadays, a selection of books narrate vivid recollections of professional musicians and entertainers, shop-owners and barmaids, policemen, and others who worked in this street's establishments and its whereabouts. Arguably, the most complete account is to be found in *Strait Street – Malta's Red-Light District Revealed* (2013) by John Schofield and Emily Morrissey.

> *In those days Malta was very strictly ruled by the Roman Catholic Church where they censored all newspapers and magazines to remove anything in the least bit risqué or controversial. Contraceptives were banned and Maltese women could be prosecuted or imprisoned for using them. It always struck me as incongruous that on the other hand the authorities turned a blind eye to the immoral goings-on of 'The Gut'.* —John Wiseman, Royal Malta Police.

Currently, 'The Gut' is undergoing a thorough regeneration programme to restore it back to its original glory. Delightful bars, restaurants, and shops are sprouting in this area in the hope of recreating a contemporary melting-pot of intriguing charm, encounters, and experiences. In the evenings Strait Street becomes a fashionable place once more!

Unearthed at Xagħra, these nine peculiar stone figures with very unusual shapes are completely different from the typical Neolithic works.

29

THE SHAMAN'S CACHE
The Xagħra Stone Circle Figures, Gozo

The discovery of a cluster of strange ancient stone figures, known as the 'Shaman's cache', at the Xagħra Stone Circle, in Xagħra, Gozo, reawakened the enigmatic allure of this prehistoric burial site. For many years, this area had baffled several scholars as they tried to locate it after it had drifted into oblivion when it was refilled in 1826 by Otto Bayer who had excavated it at the time. The only haunting clues of this site's existence were available in two illustrations which were made by Jean-Pierre Houël in the eighteenth century and by Charles de Brocktorff during Bayer's excavations. Eventually, the area was reidentified in 1964 by Joseph Attard Tabone.

Although this site had already been investigated in the nineteenth century, archaeologists Dr Simon Stoddart and Dr Caroline Malone still succeeded to uncover some remarkable findings during the excavations between 1987 and 1994. Among the most peculiar were nine stone figures with very unusual shapes and completely different from the typical works of the period. Eight of these figures were anthropomorphic representations, while one looked like a sort of animal with tusks.

In contrast with the usual rounded human figures that were generally provided with limbs, six of these statuettes, which had an average height of 20 cm, only had a human head and a

Charles F. de Brocktorff's watercolour of the Xagħra Stone Circle (1829). The site was subsequently filled in and its exact location forgotten, until rediscovered by Joe Attard Tabone in 1964.

schematic body. Two were decorated with pleated skirts and one wore a headband; none had any visible sexual characteristics. Although the figurines are uniform in appearance, none are identical, and some seemed to be left unfinished. They were not free-standing but could be placed upright in the soil and they could be easily grasped and carried around.

The other three figures were practically shaped with a head sitting on a stand. Yet even these varied from one another. One had a human head atop a small column and a pedestal. Another showed a human head resting on two legs. The third, by far the most singular, consisted of an animal's head supported on a short column.

Interestingly, when these intriguing statues were unearthed, they were found closely packed together, as if they had been originally stored in some form of container. Today, they still stand together in one of the displays at the Ġgantija Interpretation Centre, a short distance away from where they were unearthed. Some scholars believe that these statues could have been used for ritual purposes. However no one has yet identified the meaning or the function behind these alluring statuettes.

30

A TIMELESS SEA MONSTER

Sharks Around Malta

In a small archipelago like that of the Maltese Islands, where the surrounding sea is vast and boundless, one would expect to find legends and myths that relate to fantastic creatures lurking in the deepest abysses. One such folk tale describes the *silfjun* or 'fierce shark', which preys on humans. Although many tend to believe that this menace is only a figment of the imagination, there is evidence of sporadic cases which show that, from time to time, such a foreboding presence becomes terribly real. In the past, the Maltese also referred to the great white shark as *silfjun*.

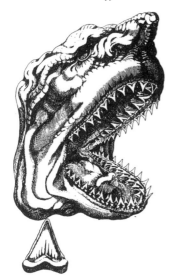

The earliest evidence of the existence of such a gruesome creature goes back millions of years in the shape of fossil teeth which belonged to the colossal prehistoric Megalodon shark. Such fossils that were discovered in the local limestone sediments suggest that this shark might

Illustration taken from Michele Mercati (1717) showing shark's head (*Carcharodon carcharias*) and teeth whose fossils found in Malta were believed to be miraculous tongues of St Paul embedded in rock.

have reached a length of 18 metres and was therefore one of the largest and most powerful predators. In Maltese tradition, these fossils have become known as St Paul's tongue, owing to their resemblance to a large tongue, and also to the belief that they were an antidote to poison. Specimens of these teeth currently form part of the collection of the National Museum of Natural History in Mdina. In fervent Pauline medieval and Hospitaller Malta, fossilized shark's teeth found in Maltese rock were thought to be impressed replicas of Saint Paul's tongue. So powerful was his preaching and conversion of the island from paganism to Christianity that his 'tongue' not only penetrated the Maltese hearts but the Maltese rock too.

Records of the *silfjun* are found in several sources. In some antique maps of Malta, dating between the late 1500s and the early 1600s, a whale-sized shark is portrayed off Filfla. In *Della Descrittione di Malta*, Giovanni Francesco Abela wrote that, in 1642, a terrifying marine monster with double rows of teeth was washed ashore at Mellieħa Bay following a storm. The German scholar Athanasius Kircher (1602–1680), after he visited Malta, describes a monstrous sea devil he had witnessed on the sands of Mellieħa Bay and asks, 'Why did nature want such monsters to exist?'

Folklore has it that a local fisherman fishing in this very same area, known as It-Trunċiera, reported that an enormous

tentacle crept up on land right behind him. This tentacle was

The *silfjun* is represented in a series of antique Maltese maps. In this map of 1577, the deep sea off Filfla plays home to giant sea monsters like the great white behemoth caught in 1987. (courtesy: Joseph Schirò)

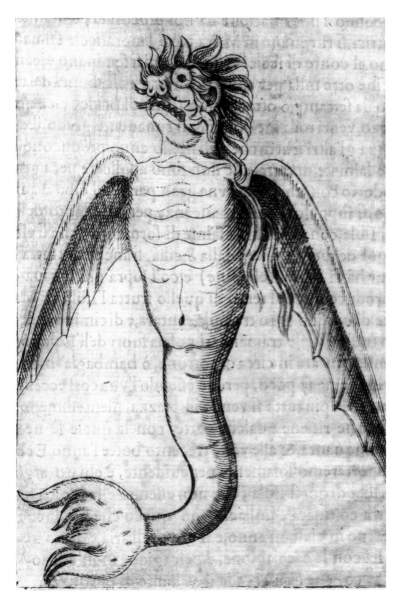

The terrifying marine monster with double rows of teeth washed ashore at
Mellieħa Bay described by G.F. Abela in 1647. (courtesy: Joseph Schirò)

so huge that it indicated that the octopus must have measured close to ten metres across!

In 1890 a large fish weighing more than 600 kg was captured in Mellieħa just a few days after two Maltese fishermen were reported to have been killed by a large shark off Marsaskala bay. The victims, Salvu Bugeja, father, aged 66, and his son, Wistin (Agostino), aged 22, were in the company of two other fishermen (also a father and his son) when their caïque (a fishing boat similar to a *luzzu*) was capsized by a large fish that the boy had spotted moments earlier. The sea creature then devoured Salvu and his son before the horrified eyes of their companions and a few others who were fishing in the

Votive painting painted by S. Portelli and offered by the fishermen Carmelo Delia and Carmelo Abela who are seen being rescued by the crew of another caïque after their boat had been attacked by a large fish (note the large fins) and devoured their companions early in the morning of 25 April 1890, some seven miles away from harbour. (courtesy: Żabbar Sanctuary Museum)

A photo of the record-breaking catch taken on 17 April 1987 at Wied iż-Żurrieq.

vicinity. This incident was witnessed by Ġużeppi Carabott and recounted by Lino Psaila in his book *Il-Baħar Rasu Iebsa*. The survivors dedicated an ex-voto (votive painting) to Our Lady which can still be viewed at the Żabbar Sanctuary Museum.

In 1956 Jack Smedley, a 40-year-old retired British navy officer, was attacked and carried away by a shark whilst swimming at St Thomas Bay in Marsaskala. A plaque in this bay still commemorates this tragedy.

Along the years, there were occasional instances when local fishermen state to have seen or captured such extraordinary fish. The most renowned of these episodes took place in 1987.

Early in the morning on 17 April of that year, Maltese fisherman Alfredo Cutajar towed in what is considered to be the biggest great white shark ever caught. Estimated at 7.14 m

The 3-ton shark being hoisted out of the water in Marsaxlokk.

Alfredo Cutajar, who in 1987 caught the largest great white shark ever recorded.

(23.4 ft) long and weighing 3 tons, the female shark had recently given birth. Inside her bowels they found a 2 m blue shark, a 2.5 m dolphin (in two pieces), and a 70 cm turtle. The shark was caught east of Filfla using hooks on float intended to catch tuna and swordfish.

This was the second time Cutajar landed a great white: his exploits earned him the nickname 'Son of God'. Photos of this phenomenal catch can be seen in several coffee shops and restaurants at Wied iż-Żurrieq.

31

AN OFFBEAT PLAY OF THE SEA

Il-Milgħuba

In December 2008, people were astounded to observe the sea suddenly rushing up the beach at Għadira (Mellieħa Bay), reaching as far as the road, then ebbing out into the bay for a notable distance, before once more flowing back up on the sand. Memories of the terrible Indian Ocean tsunami of 2004 were too uncomfortably clear and a tremor of fear ran through the onlookers. However, local fishermen were aware that there was nothing to worry much about since this was quite a common phenomenon in Maltese coastal waters and which was known as the *milgħuba*, 'seiche', or 'meteotsunami'.

Flooding at Marsaskala Bay following a *milgħuba* event in 2010. (image © TVM Joe Agius and Ivan Gouder)

Prof. Aldo Drago, a local expert in physical oceanography, remarked that the 2008 occurrence was higher in extent than other recorded episodes. He explained that such strong sea-level oscillations look very similar to tsunami waves in behaviour yet their origin is completely unrelated to seismic activity. They are triggered by particular atmospheric conditions which he describes as a large hammer striking the surface of the water and starting as a much smaller wave in the open sea which becomes greatly magnified as it approaches shallow waters.

The *milgħuba* has been noted to take place all along the northern coast of the Maltese archipelago. It generally manifests itself for only a few minutes and may occur throughout the whole year, though some seasonal characteristics are evident.

The highest seiche amplitudes are noted in March, May, and September, whereas the strongest take place in the summer months, particularly in July and August. Seiche frequency is lowest during summer and highest in winter.

Msida on the morning of 12 May 2016, when the water rose to more than a metre in level. (image © TVM Joe Agius and Ivan Gouder)

On 12 May 2016, the sea level in Msida rose over a metre, resulting in the flooding of the roads along the coast. At St George's Bay in Birżebbuġa, this phenomenon occurs on a small scale but on a regular basis, causing quite a nuisance to car users. On 10 July 2014, a moderate *milgħuba* hit the low-lying east coast, flooding bays such as Marsaxlokk, St Julian's, Msida, and Marsaskala. Eyewitnesses said that the waters receded by about a metre before the sea came flooding steadily back. Moored boats rocked and knocked into each other while bathers where confounded when the water rose quickly from their knees to their chests.

Some people refer to these non-tidal, short-period, sea-level fluctuations as 'death waves' since they may create hazards and imperil navigation. Nonetheless, this natural phenomenon also serves as an important means for the flushing of coastal inlets and harbours. Although meteotsunamis are a global phenomenon, different peoples around the world tend to give them different names. In Malta, the word *milgħuba* originates from the Maltese verb *lagħab* which means 'to play', thereby presenting these bizarre waves as the 'play of the sea'.

32

A GARDEN OF SECRETS
Villa Frere and the Lion Pit, Tal-Pietà

Walking or driving along the grounds of St Luke's Hospital in Tal-Pietà, a site overlooking the Msida yacht marina and the inner reaches of Marsamxett Harbour, one will come across a strange, yet dignified, old structure that looks rather out of place. Though in much need of restoration, its pure Doric-styled architecture still commands attention. This Neo-Classical gazebo, or *tempietto*, once stood proudly in the midst of a lush garden. A large Masonic eye sculpted in the ceiling glares down at the viewer and at the hideous dark tarmac which now completely divides the structure from its garden and which entombs a deep fissure that had aroused great public interest when it was discovered.

Back in the nineteenth century, this area was a vast stretch of garigue located at the back of Villa Frere, an unpretentious residence which faced Msida, Ta' Xbiex, and Marsamxett Harbour. It was a desperate attempt to overcome the grief brought about by his wife's death which led John Hookham Frere, a British diplomat, poet, scholar, and philanthropist, to acquire this land in order to transform it into a delightful garden, and endow it with exotic trees and flowers. He further enhanced his estate with a number of refined constructions which included two temples, pergola-walks, fountains, and numerous cisterns.

Opposite: Halfway through the gallery that leads to the pit at Villa Frere.

Marina Street, Tal-Pietà, in 1926 showing Villa Frere, then the residence of the Price family.

Frere poured all his devotion and passion into this site. In return, he was rewarded with an unexpected discovery when, in 1839, his workers came upon a large funnel-shaped fissure that was full of clay. Excavations of this funnel led to a depth of 19 metres, at which point, no further investigation was possible as the sea-level was reached and water kept flooding it. Yet Frere was not going to be disheartened easily about this find, especially since during these excavations, his workers had unearthed a cylindrical stone which was clearly carved by human hand and appeared to pertain to the prehistoric period. So far, this ancient stone's whereabouts have proved elusive.

> ... *among the stones that had been rubbed and rounded by the whirling waters, a harder piece of stone, undoubtedly worked by human craftsmanship, was found at a depth of 15 feet.* —
> Translation from Latin inscription by John Hookham Frere, 1839.

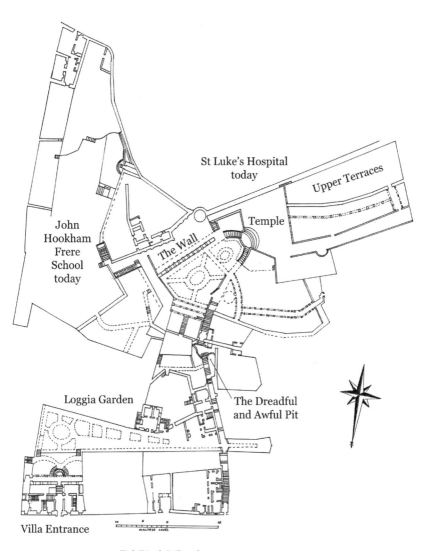

A plan of Villa Frere and its extensive gardens showing the location of the pit.
(courtesy: Friends of Villa Frere)

Opposite: The entrance to the 'dreadful and awful pit'. Above: Looking out from the innermost part of the tunnel.

This discovery was the cause of great sensation after Frere wrote about it and invited scholars to go to study it. His friend Giorgio Grognet de Vasse, the architect of the remarkable Mosta dome, suggested that this find might confirm the long-time speculations that the islands formed part of the submerged continent of Atlantis. Deeply enthusiastic about this, Frere dug a gallery to this mysterious abyss, providing access to the public.

After Frere's death, the following owner of the villa, Captain Edward Price, seems to have fallen under the same spell cast by the huge garden. In fact, after finding it completely abandoned, he dedicated much of his time to restore it back to its former glory and to add a cactus garden and a Japanese garden which included a stream, a footbridge, a pagoda gateway, stone lanterns, a Buddha shrine, and a plum tree. He also introduced some unusual fauna, the most notable of which was a pet cheetah which he kept in a pit. In a booklet on Villa Frere,

Above: The elegant Neo-Classical *tempietto*, designed by Sir George Whitmore
*c.*1910, with Capt. Price on the steps. (courtesy: Friends of Villa Frere)
Below: The temple today.

The large Masonic eye sculpted in the ceiling of the *tempietto*.

Captain Price describes the fissure discovered by Frere as the 'dreadful and awful pit'.

The phenomenal garden of Villa Frere gained international attention; distinguished visitors included British Dowager Queen Adelaide and Queen Mary of Romania. Sadly, this garden was severely bombed during the Second World War, and most of what remained was destroyed in the early 1950s to make way for the construction of Pietà Primary School and the extension of St Luke's Hospital.

The destruction of such a unique garden has been termed as shameful by architect and historic buildings conservation expert Edward Said who founded the voluntary organization 'Friends of Villa Frere'. Said is currently seeking to preserve what little has survived. In particular, the elimination of the Japanese section was one of the saddest losses for Malta's horticultural heritage, since it was the only known garden of its kind in the country. All that is left today is the dying stump of the plum tree and some stone fragments of the Buddha shrine.

33

HOLY WOOD

The Crucifix-Shaped Tree, Rabat

On the way up to Rabat, Malta, just after the road forks to Ħaż-Żebbuġ, there is a strangely trimmed tree standing upright in a concrete base. Probably, there will also be a vase of flowers and some burning candles next to it, since for many years, this tree has been considered to be miraculous.

According to local folklore, this Aleppo pine tree was once struck by lightning and suddenly the heart of its old trunk started to contort and transform, until it metamorphosed into the shape of Jesus hanging on the cross. From then on, it began to attract the devotion of Maltese believers who visited this place regularly to pray and to place flowers and candles.

As years went by, the tree became so popular that it turned into a tourist attraction. Soon, a controversy emerged between those who insisted that this tree possessed supernatural powers and those who thought that such beliefs were ridiculous and nothing less than absurd superstition and idolatry. Nevertheless, nothing stopped individuals from continuing to take care of this tree and to cherish it profoundly.

Decades passed and the renowned crucifix tree became one of Rabat's landmarks. Many were sure that this tree would live forever, and so it was quite shocking for them to see it uprooted by strong winds in 2008. Phone calls inundated the authorities demanding immediate action to save this beloved tree and this

Left: The tree before it was moved opposite, farther up the road (right).

matter was temporarily resolved after support structures were erected to support the tree in place.

However, it seems that the tree was doomed since a few months later in 2009, another heavy storm uprooted this tree once again, leading to its sad end. Ironically, several other trees standing beside it did not suffer similar consequences.

Although some thought that this tree's existence was over, it was rescued by the authorities who pulled it out of its place, cleaned it and trimmed its branches, provided it with a concrete base, and put it in the same road, close by to where it originally stood. Up to today, the crucifix tree still stands as a monument of endless faith and hope.

34

HEADS FOR CANNON SHOT

The 1565 Great Siege Atrocities, Grand Harbour

The Great Siege of Malta, which took place between May and September 1565, was one of the bloodiest conflicts witnessed by the islands. It involved the spectacular clash between the mighty force of the Ottoman Empire and the grand Order of St John which was ruling Malta. The mastermind behind this campaign was none other than Suleyman I, 'the Magnificent'. He set out to annihilate the Knights of St John, who, for hundreds of years had been harassing the Ottomans by attacking their fleets and shipping lanes.

A seventeenth-century painting of The Great Siege of Malta by an unidentified artist.

Thousands of Ottoman soldiers converged in Malta with a huge armada and a terrifying arsenal that boasted the most powerful cannon of the day. They had projected that a small island like this would be taken over in a few days.

Grand Master Jean de Valette was adamant that he would never surrender and he urged his people to fight till the end. If need be, the knights were ready to perish on this island.

Although vastly outnumbered, the knights and the Maltese bravely held back the enemy onslaught for longer than the Ottomans had envisaged. Nonetheless, on 23 June, after a month of desperate fighting, Fort St Elmo fell and almost all the surviving Christian defenders who were left inside, some barely managing to stand, were butchered.

Barbarity reached new heights when the Ottomans tied the corpses of Christians, some of which with missing body parts, to wooden planks and threw them into the sea so that

Opposite: Grand Master de Valette in the thick of battle. Below: Detail from the Grand Master's palace frescoes showing the Ottomans moving the decapitated bodies downstream towards their comrades in arms.

Robert Caruana Dingli, *Butchered Heroes of Fort St Elmo.*

the current could drift them towards Birgu where they could be seen by their comrades.

These horrible tactics were meant to terrorize the knights and the Maltese, hoping that they would surrender. Already deeply distressed by the loss of Fort St Elmo and their comrades, the knights unleashed their anger on a number of Ottoman prisoners. They beheaded them, loaded the severed heads into a cannon, and fired them into the Turkish lines.

It was a gruesome and strange episode in the course of a bitter siege which ended in September 1565, after a Christian relief force arrived in Malta and the Ottomans fled from the islands.

35

PATRIOTISM GALORE

A World Record of Five National Days

The tiny island Republic of Malta holds a world record of five national days (read holidays). An enduring controversy to reduce this number to just one has, till now, led to nothing, as various factions keep proposing different dates. The main problem is that these particular dates have been imbued with political implications and reaching a national consensus on just one of them has proven elusive, if not impossible.

31 March, known as Freedom Day, is one of the national days since it commemorates the departure of the British forces from the islands on 31 March 1979. On this day these islands did not remain a military base of a foreign power any longer.

7 June is another national day that marks the bloodiest step towards self-rule and independence for Malta. On 7 June 1919, following periods of political unrest, the Maltese rose against an oppressive British colonial administration and demanded some form of representative government for the island. A series of riots ensued and British troops fired into the crowd, killing four men.

8 September commemorates two national events. The earliest one dates back to 8 September 1565 and is known as Victory Day, since on this day the Maltese people together with the Knights of St John emerged victorious following a brutal

The Freedom Day Monument in Vittoriosa (Birgu).

The Independence Monument in Floriana.

four-month siege of the island by the Ottoman Turks. On the other hand 8 September 1943 highlights another Victory Day, this time to the lifting of the second great siege of Malta when, after 2 years of merciless bombing of the islands by Hitler's and Mussolini's air forces, news reached the island that Italy had officially surrendered. Effectively, this was the end of the war for Malta.

21 September is the national day which celebrates the independence of Malta that took place in 1964. This agreement materialized after several discussions and negotiations with the United Kingdom. Under the new constitution, Queen Elizabeth II remained the head of state represented locally by a governor-general.

13 December marks the day when Malta became a Republic in 1974. The Maltese Constitution was amended accordingly;

as a result Sir Anthony Mamo was appointed the first president of Malta.

Malta leads the pack as far as national revelry and patriotism go. The runners-up are the Netherlands, Hungary, Slovakia, Slovenia, and South Korea, with three days each. Interviewed about this situation, the former president of Malta George Abela argued that a country with five national days was a painful visible sign of disunity and political immaturity.

Although agreeing with this view, Maltese anthropologist Ranier Fsadni has pointed out that if the Maltese are unable to decide on a national day rationally, it would be better to let the pain show, rather than hide it beneath the compulsory choice of a single national day.

On the other hand, Oliver Friggieri, president of the Foundation for National Festivities, insisted about the importance of having one national day in Malta which would unite the Maltese. In his opinion, none of the existent dates should be considered but a new one has to be reinvented so that it will be free from any political fingerprints of any political party and other interests.

36

TRACES OF A DEMONIC VILLAGE

The Maqluba Sinkhole, Qrendi

Tempest Street skirts the village of Qrendi and ends right at the Tal-Maqluba area. The beautifully restored Tal-Maqluba Square brings in focus the old church of St Matthew which incorporates within it an even older shrine.

Legend says that it was here that the only remaining good woman of the village had gone to pray. The inhabitants of this hamlet had turned their backs on God and He told this woman to warn them to change their ways but no one heeded these words. On 23 November 1343, angels were dispatched to

St Matthew church, Qrendi. To the left is the staircase leading to the sinkhole.

Above: The Maqluba sinkhole with St Matthew church to the right and Filfla visible out at sea. Below: The perfectly circular Maqluba hole.

dispose of this place. A severe tempest broke out as the angels ripped the village from the roots of the earth and dumped it away at sea, creating the islet of Filfla which can be seen a short distance away. No one was spared on that day except the pious woman and nothing remained of this ungodly village but an enormous circular depression and the little church where she had come to pray, left strangely perched on its edge.

There are other myths relating to this peculiar sinkhole at Tal-Maqluba, which in Maltese means 'turned upside down'. Some say that the disappearance of the village and its demonic people was the work of the devil, whilst others claim that it was due to a huge giant who scooped up the hamlet and threw it far out at sea.

On the other hand, those who have moved away from supernatural or legendary explanations, suggest that this area might have subsided after the collapse of a large cave's

A view from inside the hole towards the steps leading down to it.

Opposite: *Macklouba*, coloured lithograph by Oliver R. Aldworth.
Above: Tal-Maqluba and St Matthew church on the saint's feast day in 1664 by Willem Schellinks.

roof which was situated beneath the limestone surface of this particular site.

This doline is a unique example in Malta and it is further distinguished since it is superimposed onto the main tributary of Wied Babu, dividing it into two: Wied San Mattew and Wied Ħal Lew. It is approximately 15 m deep and has an area of around 6,000 m² and a perimeter of 300 m.

Besides serving as a natural water reservoir, the Maqluba sinkhole acts also as a sanctuary to a number of endemic trees, insect species, and birds. Owing to its significance, the area was scheduled as a Level 1 Area of Ecological Importance and a Level 1 Site of Scientific Importance in 2008.

No matter the explanation, one can't help feeling a sort of awe, possibly mingled also with a sense of foreboding, whilst going down the rugged steps located at the left-hand side of the church which lead to a vantage point from where to admire the sinkhole.

37

WHERE THE STREETS HAD NO NAME
The Manderaggio, Valletta

The apartments and housing blocks which surround Mattia Preti Square in Valletta overlooking Fort Manoel appear rather unremarkable. Yet these structures were built over the rubble of a former notorious district of the capital, known as the Manderaggio.

Ralph Micallef, an 85-year-old local, remembers his visits in this district, both as an altar boy and as a postman later on.

As I descended the dark, long, and narrow staircase which led to the Manderaggio, I always got the impression that I was stepping into a different underground world. Many people avoided this area since it was believed to be a cove of criminals. In reality, this place was inhabited by a group of people who were not unlike anybody else, except for the hard life which they led and the dire conditions which they had to deal with each day.

The original construction of the Manderaggio goes back to the sixteenth century when the Order of St John began excavating this area to create an artificial basin to be used as a galley port. However, this project was abandoned when it was realized that the stone, which was being used to build the houses in Valletta, was unsuitable for construction purposes. Soon, people who went to seek work in the new city descended

Opposite: Some of the Manderaggio's alleys were so narrow that one could touch both walls by stretching one's arms.

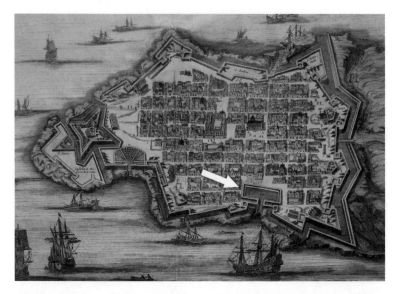

The planned artificial harbour (or *Mandracchio*) that never was, seen here in an early map of Valletta. The discarded quarry later became the ignominious slum. (courtesy: Stephen Degiorgio)

down this discarded quarry and moved into haphazardly-built hovels. Before long, an unplanned mass of slum dwellings mushroomed in the shadows of grand and noble palazzi. By the twentieth century, 333 residences were officially recorded, though it is believed that there were much more.

> *The Manderaggio was located within the area of St Patrick Street, St Mark Street, Marsamxett Street, and St Lucy Street. Its main entrance was along a staircase in St John Street, whilst two other secondary passageways were found in the streets of St Mark and St Lucy.* —Ralph.

For many years, the Manderaggio residents had no drainage arrangements except for covered holes in which to throw away natural waste. Nor did they have any water facilities in their homes. It was only in 1615, after Grand Master Alof de Wignacourt built an aqueduct which conveyed water from

A view from St Mark Street down St Patrick Street. To the left was the staircase that led down to the Manderaggio.

One of the lowest parts of the infamous quarter, sunk four storeys below the ramparts and with a total of eight storeys below the sun-baked rooftops. In heavy downpours, this culvert, that cut through Marsamxett Curtain and flowed into the sea, would relieve the Manderaggio's lanes of flooding.

Bird's-eye view of the Manderaggio. In contrast to the planned grid-like streets of Valletta, the Manderaggio had very narrow and serpentine alleys where the sunlight rarely shone on the lower floors. (courtesy: Michael Cassar)

natural water sources near Rabat, that this sunken district could avail itself of two communal water fountains.

In contrast to the planned grid-like streets of Valletta, the Manderaggio had very narrow and erratic alleys. Even the buildings themselves varied from each other, with some reaching a height of eight storeys.

> *On some occasions, when someone died in the Manderaggio, I used to accompany the priest in the Holy Viaticum procession. I remember clearly that many houses had very wide windows from which the deceased could be brought down in their coffin tied to a rope, since it was not possible to get them out from the main door as the opposite buildings were too close.* —Ralph.

In the Manderaggio, the entire drama of human life played out on the streets. The average population was evenly distributed with 2.2 persons per room. In some instances as many as seven, or even eight, people lived in one room.

Left: This communal fountain on the wall was one of two built by Grand Master Wignacourt in 1615. Right: The Order's fountain replaced by service water stand, pipe, and tap.

The Manderaggio people were quite reserved but Ralph, who got acquainted with them particularly when he worked as a postman, has very fond memories of them.

> *'Here's the postman!' the children used to call out as soon as they saw me, whilst they asked me for whom the letters were. There were no street names in the Manderaggio but only door numbers. So it was very difficult to find someone if the residents themselves didn't lead you to the correct place.*

In the British Period, sailors and foreigners who found themselves in this area, particularly when drunk, claimed that they had been robbed of everything they had. As a result many people were afraid to go down in the Manderaggio. Yet those who knew these people intimately insist that they were very

When someone died in the Manderaggio... the deceased could be brought down in their coffin tied to a rope, since it was not possible to get them out from the main door as the opposite buildings were too close.—Ralph Micallef, former postman at the Manderaggio.

religious and were particularly devoted to Our Lady of Mount Carmel. This location also boasted the origin of some of the best local bakers and musicians.

During the Second World War, many houses in the Manderaggio collapsed in the bombing. Then, in 1947, architect Dominic Mintoff, the Minister of Public Works and Reconstruction (and later Prime Minister of Malta), decided to demolish these old buildings to construct new accommodations with modern facilities for the Manderaggio residents. However, not everyone appreciated this change and Mintoff was even threatened personally and had to seek the security of the police.

Before this area was completely dismantled, Rużar Calleja, a labourer with the Department of Public Works, was asked to construct a detailed model of the Manderaggio which is today exhibited at the Inquisitor's Palace in Birgu.

Curiously, the Valletta Manderaggio was also mentioned in the adventure book *Mathias Sandorf* which was written by the French author Jules Verne in 1885. This is how Verne described this quarter:

The Manderaggio runs along under the ramparts with narrow streets where the sun never shines, high yellow walls irregularly pierced with innumerable holes, which do duty as windows, some of them grated and most of them free. Everywhere round about are flights of steps: leading to veritable sewers, low gate-ways, humid, sordid, like the houses of a Kasbah, miserable court-yards, and gloomy tunnels, hardly worthy of the name of lanes. And at every opening, every breathing-place, on the ruined landings and crumbling footpaths, there gathers a repulsive crowd of old women with faces like sorceresses, mothers dirty and pallid and worn, daughters of all ages in rags and tatters, boys half-naked, sickly, wallowing in the filth; beggars with every variety of disease and deformity; men, porters, or fisher folk of savage look capable of everything evil, and among this human swarm, a phlegmatic policeman, accustomed to the hopeless throng, and not only familiarized, but familiar with it! A true court of miracles, but transported into a strange underworld, the last ramifications of which open on to the curtain walls on the level of the Quarantine Harbour, and are swept by the sun and sea breeze.

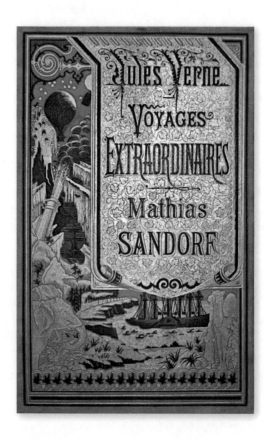

Published in 1885, *Mathias Sandorf*, Jules Verne's epic Mediterranean adventure featuring the Manderaggio forms part of 'The Extraordinary Voyages' series. In this book, Verne describes the Manderaggio as 'a true court of miracles'. This French expression referred to the slum districts of Paris, where unemployed beggars faked terrible injuries and disease when soliciting alms but dropped their characters and 'healed miraculously' once back in the slum.

38

AN UNBEARABLE MORTIFICATION

The *Dgħajsa* vs the Gondola, Venice

Time has taken its toll over Salvatore Formosa's treasured green Maltese *dgħajsa* which is being restored at the stores of the Malta Maritime Museum. However, this deceivingly humble-looking boat, is said to have once caused much embarrassment to the Venetians when it succeeded to beat the famous gondola in a race in the Venetian lagoon itself.

Liam Gauci, the curator at the Malta Maritime Museum, explains that throughout the past two centuries, Maltese

HMS *Surprise* in Venice.

boatmen and their traditional boats were common sights in Maltese harbours but it was certainly unusual to see such boats in the Venetian lagoon.

The opportunity for Salvatore, known as *Pasalv*, to use his boat in this historic lagoon had been offered to him by the commander-in-chief of the Mediterranean Fleet, when he selected him as the official boatman for his despatch vessel HMS *Surprise*. During the late 1950s, *Pasalv* was in charge of transporting officers and dignitaries to and from the ship in various ports.

One can imagine that this unique green boat, moored amongst the black gondolas next to the Doge's Palace in Venice, would have attracted much attention, particularly that of the

Salvatore Formosa, known as *Pasalv*, with his boat in the Venetian lagoon.

The Venetian gondola.

other gondoliers. It is said that in 1964 a Venetian gondolier remarked that this strange boat was too heavy to race (the ship's log, however, sees her visiting Venice in 1961, 1962 and 1963, and not 1964).

Pasalv, who was so proud of his boat which he always kept in ship-shape condition, could not accept these remarks, and he challenged the best Venetian gondolier to a race. All the gondoliers were sure that the gondola would beat the clumsy-looking foreign boat. One can only imagine the Italians' surprise and horror when the Maltese boat beat their gondola by no less than two lengths!

To their utter embarrassment, the Venetians had been defeated in their own lagoon. So great was the Venetian mortification that, the next time the HMS *Surprise* called at Venice, the harbour authorities did not allow the Maltese *dgħajsa* to be launched in the lagoon.

39

POSSIBLE SCAR OF AN IMPACT CRATER

A 'Crater' in Baħrija

No one knows exactly when the small church of St Martin in Baħrija was constructed, although some suggest that it dates to the fifteenth century. Generally, this old structure stands in sheer tranquillity and peacefulness, except during the feast of the saint when many people turn up to celebrate the occasion.

Interestingly, this church also marks the location of a strange geological feature which some believe to be the scar of

Opposite: A bird's-eye view over the 'crater'. Below: The church of St Martin in Baħrija.

Above: A view of the 'crater' from the northeast showing the almost circular fertile plain that fills this depression. Below: A view of the 'crater' from the north over Kunċizzjoni valley.

Above: A view of the 'crater' from the south with Fomm ir-Riħ and Ras il-Pellegrin in the distance. Below: A low-angle view from the east of the Baħrija depression, over the quaint St Martin church.

Above: Light enters the cave at sunset. Below: A view from inside the cave located below St Martin church.

an impact caused by a meteoroid, a comet, or an asteroid. Seen from the air, the church appears to be perched on the rim of a large, shallow crater.

Curiously, in the vicinity of this feature, there is a large cave which contains some very unusual rocks. Located both outside and inside the cave, some of these rocks are dark grey in colour, whilst others have a vitrified appearance as if, at one point in time, they had been exposed to an extremely high temperature. Yet not everyone agrees that such a calamity has ever hit this land. In fact, some suggest that this wide depression was just a sinkhole which in time filled up with sediment.

40

A DEFIANT MONUMENT

Colonna Mediterranea, Ħal Luqa

It is easy to miss this monument when driving past it, not because it is not eye-catching, but because of the palm trees that were planted around it to hide it from public view. Controversy about it ensued immediately once this phallic-shaped sculpture, called *Colonna Mediterranea*, was erected in the centre of a roundabout at the entrance to the village of Ħal Luqa in 2006. Whilst its sculptor, Paul Vella Critien, claimed that this was an avant-garde artwork that would put Malta on the artistic map, others demanded its removal, since they considered it obscene.

Matters escalated in 2010 when Pope Benedict XVI was expected to visit Malta and his route involved driving round the Ħal Luqa roundabout, where the column stands tall. Both the mayor of Ħal Luqa and the village church's authorities insisted that such a spectacle was certainly unfit to be seen for papal eyes, especially in such a Catholic country. They lobbied for its quick elimination and attracted many followers. However, others scoffed at their arguments, saying that probably, the pope would not even notice it! Indeed, this dispute gathered so much momentum that it ended as an international headline on BBC website and was also covered by CNN and *USA Today*.

Opposite: A bone of contention. *Colonna Mediterranea* in Ħal Luqa, by Paul Vella Critien.

Its sculptor insisted that his colourful elongated sculpture did not represent a phallus. Instead, it was a modern 3D representation of an obelisk that has been used since Egyptian times. He defended his work passionately and objected to its removal, whilst reprimanding his opponents for being so narrow-minded.

Eventually, the monument stayed but, when Pope Benedict XVI passed through Ħal Luqa, members of the Neo-Catechumenal Movement grouped in front of it holding a large religious banner in an attempt to hide the 'vulgar' sculpture from his view.

The story did not end there as some time later the top part of the monument was vandalized. Bickering started again on whether it was time to eliminate this abhorred column once and for all but, in the end, it was restored. It took about two-and-a-half months to complete the reconstruction and, once ready, the top part was somewhat different from how it looked originally. Many wondered how long this monument would last.

Till now, this phallic-shaped sculpture stands defiantly. The palm trees that were meant to obscure it were trimmed during the restoration process but have been purposely left to grow again to hide it from view.

Left: In 2010, a day following the government's long-overdue launch of the sexual health policy, somebody wrapped what looked like a giant condom around the controversial monument as a joke. (courtesy: *Times of Malta*)

41

BAFFLING OUTBURSTS OF ROCK
Gozo's Hillocks

For hundreds of years, Gozo has been identified by sailors as the 'island of the three hills' since these are the first visible landmarks when one approaches it by boat from Sicily. In actual fact, there are more than just three hills on the island and some of these have very peculiar geological formations. These buttes or hillocks that will be described now are anomalous isolated hills with steep sides and a round top.

Il-Qolla l-Bajda (The White Hillock), which stands singularly on the point of land that separates Qbajjar Bay from Xwejni Bay, is one of these strange outcrops. Its lower part consists of varying layers of light clay while its top part is made of pale yellow sandstone with oddly-shaped iron stones that jut out of the rock. Curiously, this hill's geology is distinctly diverse from the immediate area which surrounds it, making one wonder how it was formed.

A short distance away from Il-Qolla l-Bajda, one finds Il-Qolla s-Safra (The Yellow Hillock) which is another odd geological outgrowth. Situated slightly inland, between Qbajjar Bay and Marsalforn Bay, this hill is composed of a grey clay base and an upper layer of yellow sandstone infused with massive quartz and minerals. Again, the oddness of this hill lies in its total incongruity with the rest of the neighbouring landscape.

Opposite: The statue of Christ the Saviour on top of Merżuq Hill, Gozo.

Above: Il-Qolla l-Bajda (The White Hillock) as seen from the air. Il-Qolla s-Safra (The Yellow Hillock) lies just behind it, to the right. Below: The picturesque Xwejni Bay with the White Hillock as its focal point.

Above: Il-Qolla s-Safra (The Yellow Hillock) gets its name from its distinct yellow sandstone. Below: Il-Qolla s-Safra peeks furtively over nearby buildings.

The largest of the three hillocks, Il-Qolla tal-Merżuq.

Moreover, this formation is even more mysterious because of its atypical twisted shape which seems to allude to how this hill had been forged out of the earth.

Probably, the most popular of these weird mounds is Il-Qolla tal-Merżuq (Ray of Light Hillock) or, as it is also known, Il-Qolla tas-Salvatur (Our Saviour's Hill/Hillock) which is located amongst a series of fields between Marsalforn and Victoria. Like the other two, this hill also gives the impression to have burst out of the ground. Its core is a yellow sandstone and it has the same slanting slab top, together with a twisted semblance. According to tradition, black smoke was once seen coming out of it and this led people to believe that this was a dormant volcano. Although today there are some who still insist about this, geologists dismiss the idea as nonsense. Another legend related to this hill narrates that God once engulfed Gozo in darkness for three whole days to punish its people. Once the punishment was over, a ray of light was observed coming out of this hill.

Thereafter, a wooden cross was erected on the top of the hill which in 1904 was replaced by a statue of Christ Our Saviour. Owing to heavy weathering, this statue was replaced by another one in the 1960s but even this one was destroyed after it was struck during a thunderstorm. However, nothing seems to be able to keep the Gozitans back from having a statue of Jesus standing in this place. Presently a statue of Christ, made out of reinforced concrete, looks out protectively at passers-by from atop this enigmatic outcrop.

An interesting online article on gozonews.com from 2011 by Bruce Levine sheds light on the geographic cluster of these three outcrops. The emblem for Gozo consists of three round-topped hills with a star on top with the sea/waves below. The general consensus is that these three hills represent Nadur,

The statue of Christ the Saviour greets all who come to Marsalforn.

Detail from St George basilica, Victoria, showing the Gozo coat of arms by artist Paul Camilleri Cauchi.

Xagħra, and the Citadel (seen from the Malta side) but Levine has his doubts. According to him, if one were to approach Gozo from the north by boat, the three hillocks known as Il-Qolla l-Bajda, Il-Qolla s-Safra and Il-Qolla tal-Merżuq appear strikingly similar to the Gozo coat of arms.

He points out that Gozo's major hills are all flat-topped whereas the ones on the emblem are clearly round-topped. He also points out that anybody crossing over from Sicily could have used the three hills as markers to guide them to a safe anchorage at Marsalforn. Others discard this argument claiming that the larger hills seen from the Sicilian approach are surely, Nadur, Xagħra, and Żebbuġ.

42

THE 'MAD HOUSE'

Chateau Bertrand, Ta' Qali

In 1938, if you got through the Rabat telephone exchange and asked to get in contact with telephone no. 46, a ring would have been heard echoing around Chateau Bertrand in Ta' Qali, Ħ'Attard. Possibly the owner of this palatial building, Count Major Giuseppe Teuma-Castelletti, MVO, would have answered your call. Who knows whether his character was as grandiose as his upside-down designed house which people called 'The Mad House'?

The entrance to the 'Mad House'. Some of the palm trees that once lined this avenue are still *in situ*.

Information about Chateau Bertrand is precious and scarce. It was built in the area of Ta' Vnezja in Ħ'Attard, close to the place where today there is the Mdina Glass factory in the Ta' Qali Crafts Village. Its construction probably dates to the late nineteenth or the early twentieth century and its architect is yet unknown. A little further away from this residence, there was also a pottery factory which belonged to the same owner. This was a major industrial building in the 1920s and 1930s which produced most of the pottery manufactured in Malta.

As can be seen from surviving photos, Chateau Bertrand's design was eclectic and unorthodox and contained various architectural elements. Cylindrical turrets of different widths and heights were placed at dissociated angles along the façade, with one of them jutting high up above the house. Extravagant external winding staircases ran down unconventionally to

The bewitching rear side of Chateau Bertrand as seen across present-day Minden Grove and Vjal l-Istadium Nazzjonali from where BigMat Superstore now stands. (courtesy: Ray Polidano)

The splendidly exotic grand hall and fireplace of Chateau Bertrand. (courtesy: Ray Polidano)

greet visitors, whilst a number of disparately styled windows, doors, and arches, located at various levels, looked out like a hundred-eyed creature.

Rare photos of the internal areas of this property indicate that the house was exorbitantly decorated. A photo acquired by Raymond Polidano, Director General of the Malta Aviation Museum Foundation at Ta' Qali, shows a massive room which was richly embellished and furnished with a huge fireplace that boasted a sphinx on either side. Such photos are generally given to him by foreign war veterans who served in Malta during the Second World War and who remember Chateau Bertrand quite well. Most of them recall that it came to be known as 'The Mad House' since it had horse stables located at first floor, whilst the residence and the attic were at ground level.

Chateau Bertrand was a curio-splendour at its time and it enjoyed vast views of the surrounding countryside. This

Aerial view of Chateau Bertrand. (courtesy: Ray Polidano)

situation changed in 1938 when this zone was selected for the construction of Malta's first civil air terminal to be used by Imperial Airways. Matters got worse during the Second World War when both Chateau Bertrand and The Pottery were requisitioned to accommodate military personnel. One can only imagine the horrified reaction of Count Teuma-Castelletti when his architectural folly was turned into an RAF sergeants' mess.

Although the area was disguised to avoid being identified as an operational airfield, it was eventually recognized by the enemy, and the bizarre building of Chateau Bertrand ended up as a landmark and a target point from where to locate this zone. Soon Ta' Qali airfield was subjected to heavy bombing and it was only a matter of time before this monumental building was hit. Records provided by Susan Hudson from the official war diaries at the National Archives in London report that between 7 and 8 March 1941, JU 88s dropped bombs near Chateau Bertrand. Eventually, both Chateau Bertrand and The Pottery were damaged during the incessant bombing of the area by the enemy between March and April 1942. An entry taken from *Malta: War Diary – Diary of a George Cross* dated 6 February 1942 reads: 'Move to evacuate all sections in target area, namely Pottery and Chateau Bertrand, to caves and get caves serviceable.' Luckily, the Count had stored his stock of Maltese pottery in a safer location in a cellar at Villa Bologna in Ħ'Attard. After the end of hostilities, this craft was revived at Villa Bologna by Hon. Cecilia de Trafford and continues to this day.

Photos of the crippled Chateau Bertrand show large gaping holes in the building as the house stood shattered and forlorn

The façade facing Mtarfa. (courtesy: Ray Polidano)

for a period of time. An official entry in the Operations Record Book of the Royal Air Force Station of Ta' Qali states that both Chateau Bertrand and The Pottery were demolished completely by the British services on 1 June 1942 since they were deemed unsafe. At the site where Chateau Bertrand stood, the RAF built three joined Nissen huts which now serve as offices for P.A.R.K.S., a directorate responsible for the upkeep and maintenance of national parks and other public spaces. Only a row of palm trees which originally led to Chateau Bertrand's entrance have survived this ordeal and these may still be seen at Ta' Qali National Park, close to the amphitheatre.

Count Major Giuseppe Teuma-Castelletti, MVO, was born in 1881. He was the second son of the 3rd Count of Għajn Tuffieħa and was educated at St Ignatius College and the Malta University. He had very high connections and he served as the Colonial ADC (aide-de-camp or personal assistant)

Chateau Bertrand's owner Captain Contino Giuseppe Teuma-Castelletti (second from left), with King George V and Queen Mary during His Majesty's visit in 1912.

Above: A 1940 drawing of *The Chateau Bertrande* by Jack Whitehouse, Quartermaster of A Company, Manchester Regiment. Below: A view of the entrance avenue as seen from the house. (courtesy: Ray Polidano)

to successive governors and commander-in-chiefs of Malta between 1908 and 1918. In 1901 he married Maria Rachele Azzopardi, daughter of the 4th Baron of Buleben, and after he was widowed, he married Mary Fenech Carabott in 1941. No children were born from either marriage. Interestingly, Count Teuma-Castelletti's friendship with Lady Strickland led to some architectural changes to the magnificent Villa Bologna in Ħ'Attard. The boundary walls of the property were raised and decorated with crenels and turrets resembling mock fortifications. The Bertrand folly had extended its influence to an eighteenth-century country house. Besides Chateau Bertrand, the Count also owned other properties, including 7, Strada Reale in Valletta (Domus Zammitello), and Villa Abbandonati in Ħaż-Żebbuġ. He passed away in 1942; the same year when his surreal property was blown up and left only to memory.

Aerial view of Ta' Qali National Park with the Mdina Glass factory in the foreground and Mdina in the distance with an arrow marking the site where the eclectic house once stood.

Top, left: Count Teuma-Castelletti fired a local pottery industry in this building attached to his house. Above and right: Photos showing the house and pottery in ruins following German bombing in March 1941. (courtesy: Ray Polidano)
Below: Chateau Bertrand's location so close to Ta' Qali airfield eventually sealed its fate. (courtesy: Mark Vella, NWMA)

Yet Chateau Bertrand's story does not end here. Although many might believe to have lost the opportunity to visit this legendary house, it is curious to note that a strikingly similar building known as Villino Florio can still be found at Via Regina Margherita in Palermo. Villino Florio was constructed between 1899 and 1902 by Vincenzo Florio who came from a prominent entrepreneurial Italian family. Its design was commissioned to the notable architect Ernesto Basile (1857–1932) who was one of the pioneers of Art Nouveau in Italy and was renowned for his stylistic fusion of ancient, medieval, and modern elements. In 1962 Villino Florio was severely damaged in an arson attack but the villa was later beautifully restored and it is now open to the public.

The similarity between Chateau Bertrand and Villino Florio is remarkable since they share many identical architectural features. Could it be that they shared the same architect too?

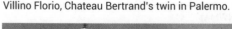

Villino Florio, Chateau Bertrand's twin in Palermo.

Spot the difference. Left, Villino Florio in Palermo. Right, Chateau Bertrand, Ta' Qali.

Villino Florio, Palermo. Architectural drawing by Ernesto Basile.

43

AN ALLURING OPEN CAVE

Dragonara Cave, Mellieħa

At the extreme northern tip of the island, a short distance away from the coastal tower known as Aħrax or The White Tower in the Aħrax tal-Mellieħa area, there is a gem of a sinkhole, technically known as a doline, that is quite unique to the islands. The cave goes by several names including Dragonara Cave, Coral Lagoon, Aħrax Hole, and Aħrax Cave. The doline was probably formed when the roof of a cave collapsed creating an elliptical pool of water that is connected to the sea via a small fissure at its southeast end. The depth of this minute inland sea is about 6 metres all around and when the sun shines straight overhead, the seabed lights up a gorgeous green.

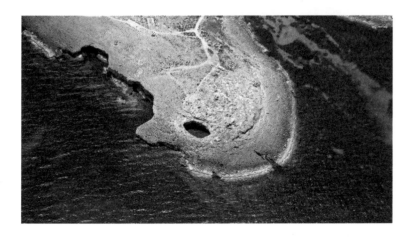

44

PATHS TO NOWHERE
The Enigmatic 'Cart-Ruts'

Many know Clapham Junction as a major railway station and transport hub in London. In Malta, the area which bears this nickname is located in a prehistoric site at Misraħ Għar il-Kbir, near Buskett. There is a baffling similarity between the complex London train tracks and the multitude of ancient 'cart-ruts' carved in the bedrock which led to this analogy. However, the correlation ends there since the real function of these features has not yet been determined.

There are several other areas around the Maltese Islands with similar worn-out 'cart-ruts' that appear to have been dug out in antiquity. Although similar phenomena are observed in other parts of the world, these features are mainly confined to the Mediterranean region. In Malta the great number of these enigmatic parallel grooves is in itself baffling.

The ancient origin of these 'cart-ruts' is clearly demonstrated by some examples which were disturbed in the Punic Period (700–218 BC) when they were cut during the construction of shafts for tombs. Likewise these features are completely ignored by the modern landscape pattern as they are buried in field soil, overlain by rubble walls, roads, buildings, or simply quarried away.

Opposite: 'Cart-ruts' located in San Pawl tat-Tarġa, limits of Naxxar.

Above: Clapham Junction railway station, Wandsworth. The multitude of tracks draws a parallel to the eponymous Maltese 'cart-ruts' located close to Buskett (below).

The number of ruts present at these sites can vary extensively and even their length presents notable contrasts, extending from a few to several metres.

The direction which these 'cart-ruts' follow is as strange as their presence. They often change course for no apparent reason while others appear and then fade away abruptly again. A few finish over the edges of sea cliffs, whilst a particular pair reach down to the seabed and continue for some distance under water. Research has shown that ruts left by recent 'cart-ruts' are quite distinct from the ancient ones. Modern ones are mainly broader and shallower, and unlike their predecessors, they present heavy wear on the surface rock in the middle, left by whatever animal was utilized to pull the cart.

Although logically these 'cart-ruts' are presumed to have served for some kind of transportation, the lack of evidence

Diverging ruts located in San Pawl tat-Tarġa, limits of Naxxar. (courtesy: Gordon Weston)

Above: An interesting pair of 'tracks' just off Clapham Junction swerving past the cave known as Għar il-Kbir. Below: An ancient quarry located close to Clapham Junction dating to c.700–500 BC.

of any organized system defies reason. Also there is nothing to reveal what objects were being carried. Their evident heavy wear in bedrock and their proximity to quarries have often led to the idea that these 'cart-ruts' could have been used to carry the large megalithic blocks required for the construction of the prehistoric temples. Yet this theory soon fails when one observes that, though there are examples of 'cart-ruts' which run near temples and quarries, none of these lead directly to a temple and only two terminate in a quarry.

Archaeologists differ on the period when these 'cart-ruts' could have been created, their estimations ranging from the Neolithic Period (5000–4100 BC), to the Temple Period (4100–2500 BC), to the times of the Order of St John (AD 1530–1798), although the Bronze Age (2400–700 BC) and the Classical Period (218 BC–AD 535) are the most favoured. So far no scientific technique has been able to date these perplexing rock cut features.

A set of deeply incised 'cart-ruts' located in San Ġwann.

Above: Aerial view showing the baffling array of converging, diverging, and intersecting 'cart-ruts' at the site known as Clapham Junction. Below: Disturbed in the Punic Period (700–218 BC), these 'cart-ruts' at Clapham Junction were broken during the construction of shafts for tombs.

45

A MIRACULOUS PLANT

The General's Root, Fungus Rock, Dwejra, Gozo

In the sixteenth century, the area of Dwejra in Gozo became renowned for a strange plant which grew on the flat top of a small islet with very high sides. Phallic in shape and boasting a blood-red colour, the plant was considered to be able to cure all ills, including erectile dysfunction, and also to instil happiness and satisfaction when worn close to a woman's heart.

Believed to grow only on this islet and nowhere else in the world, the plant soon became highly sought after. The name *Fungus melitensis* was conjured up for this plant when it was mistakenly thought to be a fungus and the islet became known as Fungus Rock.

Since it was considered to be rare, the plant became extremely valuable and many tried to climb the high rock to collect and sell it. It was so appreciated that the Order of St John even donated these plants to distinguished visitors. This plant was also used as a styptic dressing for wounds and as a medication for dysentery.

In 1652 Grand Master Jean Paul de Lascaris-Castellar built the Dwejra Tower in a strategic place to guard the coastline of Dwejra Bay against the enemy and also to deny access to the locals from obtaining this plant. These measures got stricter in 1746 when Grand Master Manuel Pinto da Fonseca decreed the islet out of bounds and posted a permanent guard on this site.

Above: Late eighteenth-century view of the isolated islet called 'Mushroom Rock' (Fungus Rock) by Jean Houel. Notice the original 'cable car' that was constructed by Grand Master Pinto. Below: The hoist system which provided gatherers with access to the precious flowering plant, erroneously called a 'fungus', from a mid-nineteenth-century painting by Sir George Whitmore.

Cynomorium coccineum or the General's Root.

He ordered the sides of the rock to be smoothened to remove footholds and constructed a hoist system between the island and the mainland to facilitate the collection of the precious plant by those responsible for this task. Trespassers were sentenced to a penalty of three years as oarsmen on the galleys.

In 1800 Sir Alexander John Ball, a British admiral and the first civil commissioner of Malta under the English rule, issued a proclamation prohibiting the collection of this plant.

Today, the Fungus Rock is a nature reserve and is inaccessible to the public although its shoreline can be reached by bathers. A great deal of confusion is related to its nomenclature as this islet is also known as the General's Rock. The plant which still grows

The rock as it stands today.

on it, although in very small quantities, also referred to as the General's Root, and the Master's Root is now known not to be a fungus but a parasitic flowering plant known as *Cynomorium coccineum* and it is being studied by pharmacologists. The plant also grows in a few other areas in very limited numbers.

46

AN ENIGMATIC ABYSS

The Ħal Saflieni Hypogeum, Paola

The various megalithic temples of Malta and Gozo form part of the enigmatic past of these islands. Yet their underground replica, which is located at Ħal Saflieni Hypogeum in Paola, is even more peculiar. Thousands of human bones were unearthed here when it was accidentally discovered in 1902. Curiously, none of these remains were preserved, except for a small number of controversial skulls which are regarded as somehow elongated and alien in appearance.

These findings led scholars to believe that this place was a prehistoric underground burial site. However, the beautifully carved features in the honey-coloured limestone, particularly those in the chamber known as the 'Holy of Holies', suggest that this structure could have served for more elaborate purposes.

Further bizarre manifestations can be observed in the Oracle Room from which one can produce unusual powerful vocal acoustic resonance by speaking through a hole dug in one of its walls. Researchers have detected the presence of a strong double resonance frequency at 70 Hz and 114 Hz, causing low voices to boom through the rooms in terrifying echo waves that last up to eight seconds. Laboratory testing indicates that exposure to these particular resonant frequencies can have a physical effect on human brain activity. Similarly puzzling is its intricately adorned ceiling with cryptic spirals painted in red ochre.

The hypogeum was one of the best-kept Maltese secrets of the early twentieth century. Prior to its official 1902 discovery, builders working on the houses located above the hypogeum had already pierced through the ceiling of this wonder of the ancient world and built supports to secure their foundations, but had kept it under wraps.
(image: Maurizio Urso; courtesy: Heritage Malta)

The Holy of Holies. The carved ceiling, imitating partial corbelling may reflect how the above-ground temples were roofed over. (image: Maurizio Urso; courtesy: Heritage Malta)

The original use of this site may be tentatively gleaned from the number of statuettes and artefacts that were recovered from the elegantly designed main chamber. Still the reason behind the creation of such artworks remains obscure.

The whole hypogeum complex is quite huge and made up of interconnecting rock-cut chambers set on three distinct levels. It must have been started in *c.*4000 BC and it seems that this site was still in use by *c.*2500 BC when its operations were suddenly interrupted. Abrupt, unfinished architectural works observed at the lowest levels of this structure indicate that there were plans to extend the area. Something must have led to the termination of this arrangement and to its immediate abandonment, followed by the brusque disappearance of any further signs of these temple builders.

In recent years, the lowest level of this hypogeum could not be accessed since it was deemed unsafe. Some insist that

A girl looks through one of the openings inside the main chamber of the hypogeum, (*c.*1975). The area in which the Ħal Saflieni Hypogeum was discovered was known as Tal-Għerien (of the caves) suggesting that this location was known for its underground spaces.

Early photograph of the Oracle Chamber. New research points to the possibility that the hypogeum possesses unique acoustic properties that have a significant effect on the human brain. (courtesy: Richard Ellis Archive)

this is a security measure against the obscure nature of this deepest section which is believed to have some tunnels leading to unknown and remote spaces. Indeed, some years ago, Lois Jessup, a British embassy worker who convinced a guide to allow her to explore this section, came out with a very intriguing story. She narrated how, after crawling through a passage, she had emerged on a cavern ledge which overlooked a deep chasm. In this abyss, she claimed to have seen a procession of tall humanoids with white hair covering their bodies walking along another ledge about 50 feet down, on the opposite wall of the chasm.

An article published in the August 1940 issue of *The National Geographic Magazine* reported that the tunnels under the Ħal Saflieni Hypogeum had been sealed off after a group of students and their teachers who had entered on a field trip had disappeared without trace. They had been roped to each other with the end of the rope being tied at the opening of the cave. As the last student

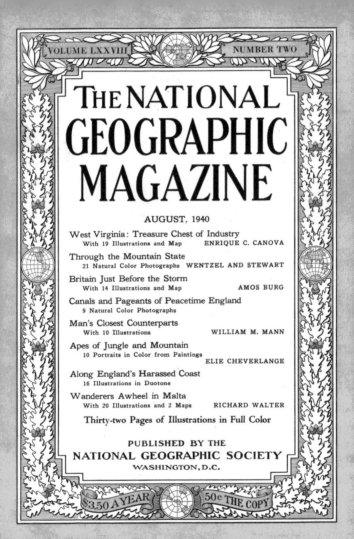

VOLUME LXXVIII   NUMBER TWO

THE NATIONAL GEOGRAPHIC MAGAZINE

AUGUST, 1940

PUBLISHED BY THE
NATIONAL GEOGRAPHIC SOCIETY
WASHINGTON, D.C.

$3.50 A YEAR   50c THE COPY

The August 1940 issue of *The National Geographic Magazine* told the story of a number of elementary school children and their teachers who descended into the hypogeum, never to return. They could be heard wailing and screaming for

The famous sculpture known as 'The Sleeping Lady', discovered in Ħal Saflieni, with her ample breasts, relatively small waist, and enormous buttocks, whose role and function continue to elude us. (courtesy: Heritage Malta)

turned the corner the rope was cut clean, the walls caved in, and all the party disappeared. For many days, the wails and cries of children were reported coming from underground in different parts of the island. Yet numerous efforts by search parties were all unsuccessful, or so the story goes.

From its first opening to the public, in 1908, this site has been visited by thousands of people and this has taken its toll on its delicate microclimate. In fact, this archaeological site, which boasts UNESCO World Heritage status, was closed between 1990 and 2000, in order to affect the required conservation procedures. Eventually, a new environmental-control system was implemented but the number of visitors was limited to 10 people an hour for not more than 8 hours a day. The Ħal Saflieni Hypogeum is unique in the history of world architecture. The phenomenon of subterranean replication of above-ground elements predates rock-cut architecture by several millenia.

47

A BLOODY IMPRESSION

Caravaggio's *The Beheading of St John the Baptist*, Valletta

No one is left unimpressed when stepping inside the solemn knights' temple of St John's co-cathedral in Valletta. Its brilliant golden interior is a gem of Baroque art and architecture which manifests the affluence and the supremacy of the Order that constructed it. Yet far more unique treasures lie within the dark recesses of its cavernous oratory.

Silence enhances the ominous and austere ambience where the knights used to hold their official ceremonies under the watchful eyes of Christian saints and heroes who looked down on them from the surrounding walls.

Here hangs the magnificent *The Beheading of St John the Baptist* which was painted by the renowned artist Michelangelo Merisi da Caravaggio (1571–1610) during his brief stay in Malta between 1607 and 1608 at the time of the magistracy of Alof de Wignacourt.

Dominant, large, and an apogee of artistic genius, this painting demands unconditional attention as it unfolds, along its expanse, the full brutality of a violent and dramatic event. It depicts the moment when John the Baptist was beheaded in prison by an order of King Herod, just before his head was placed on a platter to be presented to the kings' guests. This was the result of the deep hatred Herodias, Herod's brother's wife, harboured for the Baptist. She got wind that during the

The Beheading of St John the Baptist by Caravaggio. (image: Maurizio Urso; courtesy: St John's Co-Cathedral Foundation)

king's birthday celebrations, John had told Philip, Herodias husband, that it was unlawful for him to have her as his wife.

However, a careful observation reveals more than this gruesome scene since this is the only painting signed by Caravaggio. Several art critics have contemplated the meaning behind the frenzy of inspiration which led this controversial artist to dip his brush in the fresh blood oozing out of the saint's severed neck in order to inscribe his name. Many believe that the clue lies right within the way in which he signed, 'f(ra?) MichelAn...', which means that he is vaunting of his newly acquired status as a knight of St John.

Caravaggio knew quite well that this honour was a phenomenal achievement since he was not of noble birth and, moreover, he was a fugitive from justice for having committed murder. His turbulent past is well-recorded and he was notoriously known for his troublesome and fearless nature which often led to his arrest or imprisonment. In 1606

The Oratory dedicated to The Martyrdom of St John the Baptist.

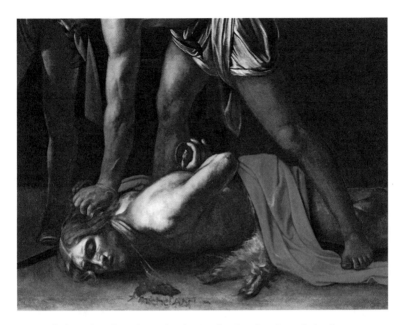

Detail of *The Beheading of St John the Baptist* showing the artist's signature.
(copyright: Maurizio Urso)

he killed Ranuccio Tomassoni in Rome and a *bando capitale* was issued against him which allowed for his beheading and the consignment of his head to the authorities.

Could this parallel fate have inspired him to uniquely scrawl his name on this one canvas? One of Caravaggio's earliest biographers, Giovan Pietro Bellori, makes a strong case for the association between the darkness of Caravaggio's style and the darkness of the artist's own personality.

Sadly, this genius of a man did not cherish this triumph for very long as he was unable to harness his own demons. Indeed, just two days before inaugurating this very painting, Caravaggio was again arrested for taking part in a fight where a man was seriously wounded. Soon, he was imprisoned in Fort St Angelo. It was only with the help of some powerful friends

Michelangelo Merisi da Caravaggio.

that he managed to escape to Sicily, leaving behind him all that he had achieved in those last months.

Ironically, the noble title for which he had yearned so much was immediately stripped away from him *in absentia* and, as the records of the Order dramatically put it, 'expelled and thrust forth like a rotten and fetid limb', in the very oratory of the conventual church of St John's, right in front of the only signed painting that he had completed just a few weeks before.

48

MIND THE GAP
Gozo's Pavements

The typical Gozo pavement, or *bankina* in Maltese, seems to defy all logic behind its actual purpose. The ambling pedestrian ought to keep an eye out, as here, the footpaths all too often do not follow the gradient of the road. Instead, they seem to conveniently prefer a level plain, at times rising to vertiginous heights of 80 cm to a metre, doubling as buffer zones for the houses abutting them, or, at an average 50 cm, perfect seating spots for those balmy summer evenings. This is not a purely Gozitan phenomenon though it seems to be more prevalent here. Local regulations state that pavements should not exceed 20 cm in height though nothing has been suggested for those summer community gatherings.

Veritable precipices called 'pavements'.

49

A CHILLING DISCOVERY

The Bones of St Gregory Church, Żejtun

For several years, the elderly of Żejtun claimed that people were buried around the dome of their old parish church of St Catherine, popularly known as St Gregory's. Various searches to locate them proved futile and many believed that this was only a legend until a remarkable discovery on 12 March 1969 confirmed they were right, but not completely. Human remains were really found in secret passages within the church. However, these passages were not located around the dome but within the walls of the church's eastern transepts, running beneath the roof.

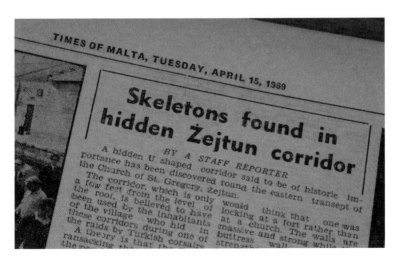

TIMES OF MALTA, TUESDAY, APRIL 15, 1969

Skeletons found in hidden Żejtun corridor

BY A STAFF REPORTER

A hidden U shaped corridor said to be of historic importance has been discovered round the eastern transept of the Church of St. Gregory, Żejtun.

The corridor, which is only a few feet from the level of the roof, is believed to have been used by the inhabitants of the village who hid in these corridors during one of the raids by Turkish corsairs ransacking the ...

The old church of St Catherine (known as St Gregory church) in Żejtun.

On 15 April 1969 the *Times of Malta* reported that John M. Debono, the sacristan of this old parish church, had accidentally identified a hidden U-shaped corridor situated just a few feet below the level of the roof. Yet, along the years, others declared to have located this site before him. These include Grezzju Vella who affirms that it was he who had discovered the opening on the roof which led to the passages and that he was the first person to be lowered down in them to explore what there was inside.

Curiously, during the 1969 discovery, two initials, V.A. and C.Z. accompanied by the date 19.2.09 were noticed scratched on a stone on the wall which lead to the third passage. These indicated that this site had already been found 60 years before. To clear this dilemma, the parish priest succeeded to locate one of the two men who had left their initials within the secret passages. Carmelo Zahra known as *ir-Rangu* revealed that he had entered these passages on 19 February 1909 together with some other people. They had found human skeletons dressed as soldiers with weapons and some small flags beside them. Zahra declared that some of the individuals that were with him took away some items and they threatened the others not to speak about this discovery, so they never did.

Still there was the question of how these human remains had ended up in these passages. Between 1979 and 1980, Seshadri Ramaswamy and Joseph Leslie Pace produced detailed reports about their paleopathological and anthropological investigations of these bones. They concluded that these remains had been originally buried in soil and later transported to these passages, thereby indicating that this site might have served as an ossuary. Yet some regard this theory as implausible and they recommend further studies to get more definitive answers.

Along with the skeletons, some other items were found. These are stored in a cabinet in the church and include a wooden shoe sole with a high heel; a small gilded wooden

Ġan Marì Debono with the human bones discovered in 1969.

Human bones discovered in the secret passages of St Gregory church. (photo: Fiona Vella)

cross of Byzantine design; odd bits of a gilded wooden frame (perhaps an icon); three coins; two of bronze with the cross of the Order, the other of gold, but very worn out; pieces of pottery of the sixteenth/seventeenth century; and some animal bones.

While cleaning up the secret passages in 1969, Debono realized that there were also five blocked loop-holes within the outer walls. When he removed the obstructions, it became clear that the narrow slits looked out at St Thomas Bay, Marsaskala, Fort St Thomas, Marsaxlokk, and Fort St Lucian. These look-outs indicated that, for a time, this church might have acted as a watchtower and that these passages were probably used by local militia.

Some days later, Debono also managed to uncover another entrance to the passages. 'He made several attempts to trace it out. Eventually he came upon a wall cupboard which was

Human bones discovered in the
secret passages of St Gregory
church. (photo: Fiona Vella)

Above: The secret passageway (photo: Fiona Vella). Below: Aerial photo from the southeast showing the old church of St Gregory (St Catherine) and the new parish church in the background. The location of the first hidden corridor is marked with an arrow.

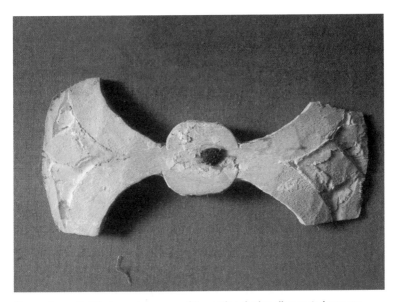

Above: A small gilded wooden cross of Byzantine design discovered among the bones. Below: A wooden shoe sole with a high heel was also found in this forgotten passage. Bottom: Three coins, two bronze and one gold, were also found among the human remains. (photos: Fiona Vella)

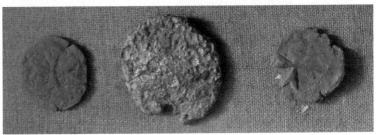

Initials and dates found engraved in the secret passages. (photo: Fiona Vella)

situated in an area along the winding staircase and seemed to be of no use. He decided to ask his friend Ġanni Vella, who was known as 'Ġanni *l-ġgant*' (Ġanni the giant), to bring one of his mason's tools; a huge iron nail with which building stones were kept in place. He knocked on the wall cupboard with this tool and suddenly, this feature moved out of the wall, revealing another entrance to these passages. It is from this entrance that people get in to view these passages nowadays,' recounted his son Charles Debono.

No one knows when this old church was built. The earliest record dates to Bishop Senatore de Mello's pastoral visit to Malta in 1436, who documented this site as the parish church of Żejtun.

50

THE ONLY WOMAN BURIED AMONGST MEN

A Grand Master's Mistress Interred in St
John's Co-Cathedral, Valletta

The austere façade of St John's co-cathedral in St John Street
in Valletta reveals nothing of the inconceivable splendour of
its interior. Visitors are simply overwhelmed at the beauty
and the richness of the place as soon as they step inside. Each
corner has its own story to tell and one visit is definitely not
enough to grasp all the details. Built by the Order of St John a
few years after the victorious end of the Great Siege of 1565 to
serve as its conventual church, this sacred building was also
used to bury within it the deceased grand masters and knights.
It was a place built by men for men and yet, very few people
know that one woman has somehow succeeded to defy this
rule by being interred amongst them.

As stated by Albert Ganado in his article 'The dismantling
of de Rohan's monument in the Conventual Church of St John'
in *Treasures of Malta* Vol. XIV No. 3, the identity of this woman
is still uncertain. She was buried at the feet of the tomb of
Grand Master Fra Emmanuel de Rohan within the chapel of
the Langue of France, which is the first chapel to the left of
the main altar of the co-cathedral. Although in his book *Turkey,
Greece and Malta* (1837) Adolphus Slade wrote that this woman
was buried in this church sometime after 1800 as a concession
by Sir Thomas Maitland since she was de Rohan's cousin,
many believe that in reality she was his mistress.

Grand Master Emmanuel de Rohan-Polduc who ruled Malta between 1775 and 1797 had a secret love affair with his own cousin.

Notwithstanding the fact that all the knights were sworn to celibacy, some of their love-affairs were no secret. Even de Rohan himself slipped this technicality when he fell in love with his cousin Marie de Rohan-Montbazon, the daughter of Prince de Guémenée. She was in her early twenties and he was in his sixties.

An article in the local newspaper *Il Portafoglio Maltese* (2 March 1839) criticized some mistakes in Slade's book, including the information related to this woman. The newspaper claimed that the deceased woman was the daughter of Countess de Rohan-Miniac who had declared that she was a relative of the grand master but had never stated that she was his sister. Apparently, in France the Countess had been convicted of fraud and was also imprisoned but when she came to reside in

The Chapel of France in St John's co-cathedral where Marie de Rohan-Montbazon, the only woman in a temple of men, allegedly lies buried. The marble mausoleum to the right belongs to Grand Master de Rohan.

Sir Thomas Maitland, the first British governor of Malta (1813–24), who allowed Marie de Rohan-Montbazon to be buried beside Grand Master de Rohan.

Malta, she had managed to obtain hundreds of pounds from Maitland. Who knows whether this Countess was the wife of Prince de Guémenée who had gone bankrupt in 1782? If that were the case, then she would be none other than the mother of Marie de Rohan-Montbazon.

Possibly someday this mystery will be resolved. The burial of this singular woman within St John's co-cathedral will always stand there challenging the norm.

51

NAME AND SHAME
The Masks of Shame

In medieval Malta and during the Knights' period, state retribution tended to be somewhat creative. Some of the punishments were especially intended to belittle people in the eyes of their neighbours and render them ridiculous. A few were extremely imaginative and there was hardly any limit to the depths of human inventiveness.

The instruments of punishment used were as numerous and varied as the offences. *Maschere d'infamia,* or masks of shame, were created in the most bizarre fashion. Most of these masks were symbolic, referring to particular offences. They consisted of a humiliating and/or painful device worn by the accused, generally on the face and head.

One such mask with big ears was made for eavesdroppers. A mask with a big mouth and a long tongue signified that everything the wearer got to know was maliciously repeated to others while a big-nosed one was intended for those who meddled in other people's business. For instance, a man, who had behaved in an inappropriate or indecent manner, was forced to wear a mask in the shape of a boar's head.

Such masks also bore inscriptions such as 'The shrew who cannot hold her tongue has to put this muzzle on.' There were also masks of shame for scamping (behaving in an unscrupulous and mischievous way) and for botching craftsmen. Many of

Some examples of masks of shame displayed at the Mdina Dungeons, Mdina. These bizarre punishment masks were as numerous and varied as the offences.

An example of a mask of shame displayed at the Mdina Dungeons, Mdina.

them covered the face completely but the condemned person never remained anonymous.

Although these masks very rarely caused physical pain, they pointed clearly to the negative side of the affected person and his misdeeds, and aroused grim feelings of what is probably the lowest and most reprehensible form of satisfaction: a pleasure in gloating over the misery of others.

52

THE EXECUTED EXECUTIONER

An Eventful Hanging at Gallows Square, Rabat

A most extraordinary event took place in Rabat in 1802, when Malta had barely experienced two years of British rule. During the night of 15 September of that year, Francesco Mariano, a Neapolitan man, stole a silver sanctuary lamp from St Publius church in Floriana. The theft of sacred objects was a grave offence at the time and carried with it the penalty of life imprsonment. During the Order of St John's rule, this most heinous of crimes would have certainly called for the death penalty.

Detail from a watercolour of an execution outside Corradino Prison in Malta in 1860. (courtesy: Albert Ganado)

Above: The name of the square reads 'Gallows Square'. Below: Misraħ il-Forok in Rabat where executions used to take place.

While Mariano was in prison, Salvu Farrugia, aged 24, was found guilty of murdering another man in a bar fight and sentenced to death. It just so happened that at the time there was no executioner in Malta to carry out the sentence. With Sir Alexander Ball's approval, the court asked Mariano whether he would be ready to carry out this unenviable task. In return, Mariano would be liberated on condition that he left Malta soon after the execution. For the hapless Neapolitan, it seemed that luck had graced him with a second chance.

On 18 October 1802, Salvu Farrugia was led to Misraħ il-Forok (Gallows Square) in Rabat (a stone's throw away from St Dominic priory, just behind St Sebastian church) where executions used to take place in the days of the Order. As was customary at the time, after the hanging, the military officer in charge would fire a shot at the prisoner's head, the *coup de grace*, to make sure that he was dead. However, on this fateful day, while the officer was drawing his pistol, it misfired and instead hit the executioner Mariano, who fell dead on the spot. The crowd walked away murmuring that God had surely punished the Neapolitan for stealing the silver sanctuary lamp.

53

TAKING THE PLUNGE
The Diving Dog at St Peter's Pool, Marsaxlokk

Located close to Marsaxlokk at the tip of Delimara Point in the Southeast of Malta is St Peter's Pool, one of the most beautiful and stunning natural swimming spots that the Maltese littoral has to offer. Rather remote and hard to access, this rocky bay is mostly frequented by locals. Until recently at least… Tourists now flock here to catch a glimpse of the duo that put St Peter's Pool on the world map.

They are Carmelo Abela and his pet, a Jack Russell Terrier called 'Titti' who became famous after a video of their perfectly coordinated synchronized dives went viral worldwide. The pup never hesitates to leap off 12-foot cliffs, perfectly breaking the surface of the water together with her loving and devoted owner. Carmelo and Titti go down to St Peter's Pool almost everyday in summer, where locals and foreigners alike will be hoping to see them perform and maybe get a picture of the famous airborne dog. Titti is a loyal dog and will only jump with her owner, Carmelo says. Totally enamoured with the sea, she barely gives him time to get off his motorbike before she runs off and leaps off the edge into the gin-clear waters. She is adored by everybody who sees her and she even has her own Facebook page.

Opposite: Carmelo and Titti leap off into the blue. (photo: Renata Apanaviciene)

Top: Carmelo and Titti emerge from the water to an applause. (photo: Renata Apanaviciene) Above: St Peter's Pool, the famous duo's aquatic stage.

One of the crowd's favourite numbers is the tandem dive; one simple gesture from Carmelo and Titti runs along the rim of the bay, off to the opposite side, and leaps into the air towards the centre of the pool together with her owner. Her total confidence is probably what strikes people the most. Carmelo says that he warmed up to idea of owning a Jack Russell after watching Jim Carrey's movie *The Mask*.

54

NUNS AND PENITENT PROSTITUTES

The Magdalene Monastery, Valletta

Unrelenting bombing of Valletta during the Second World War caused the destruction and demolition of several buildings. However, many old buildings still survive and they have interesting stories to tell. One of these is St Magdalene church which is located at the lower end of Merchants Street.

The church's narrative goes back to the seventeenth century during the rule of the Order of St John when it was built along with a monastery to welcome penitent prostitutes who took vows of chastity, obedience, poverty, and enclosure,

The Magdalene church at the bottom of Merchants Street, close to Fort St Elmo.

A kneeling Magdalene nun. (courtesy: National Library of Malta)

and became cloistered nuns. This building replaced a former monastery which was situated close to St Ursula's monastery and was deemed unsuitable to live in by Inquisitor Innocenzo del Bufalo de' Cancellieri during a visit in 1596.

Cloistered monasteries of the Magdalene nuns could be found in various countries, particularly in port areas where prostitution was strong. Malta was no exception and the situation was exacerbated with the arrival of the Order of St John in 1530 when a number of prostitutes followed them from their previous headquarters in Rhodes. Negative criticism against the Order led to the establishment of the first Magdalene monastery by Grand Master Hugues Loubenx de Verdalle in 1594. Yet prostitution remained rampant. In the seventeenth century, a Frenchman who visited Malta wrote that nowhere else in the world was it as easy to succumb to a venereal disease.

The new monastery was built in style and fine luxury and was even equipped with its own water system and fountain. The adjacent church was decorated with paintings by the most renowned artists of the time, such as Filippo Paladini and Mattia Preti. The previous critical financial condition of the monastery was dealt with by new regulations which comprised annual subsidies by the Order, financing by the Girolama Ciantar foundation, dowries brought over by the nuns, donations, and a tax of one-fifth of all the wealth left by deceased prostitutes in Malta.

These new arrangements attracted girls of richer families who decided to join this congregation, leading to an elitist system among the nuns. Whilst the higher-level nuns administered the wealth of the monastery, the subordinate nuns dealt with domestic chores, a situation that often led to conflict. Trouble also arose when the monastery's regulations were bent to cater for particular situations which at times made the nuns retaliate in a scandalous way. A case in point was when they tried to poison a pregnant girl whom they had been constrained to accept in the monastery.

Over the years, the power and influence of the Magdalene nuns increased considerably especially with the inclusion of a number of prominent women. One of these was the repentant nun Dorothea Valenti, a former mistress of Grand Master Antoine de Paule, who brought a large sum of money and her three-year-old daughter Anna with her to the monastery. Since children were prohibited from living with these nuns, Valenti made a special arrangement with Pope Urban VIII to allow the girl to stay at the monastery on condition that she became a cloistered nun at her adolescence. The girl did take the veil but she eventually obtained a dispensation from her vows and left the monastery under the name of Anna Pitard.

Extensive research by historian Christine Muscat which was published in her book *Magdalene Nuns and Penitent Prostitutes, Valletta* (2013) disclosed some other scandals that took place

The façade of the Magdalene church and monastery from a medical diploma dated 22 August 1833.

Donna Caterina Valenti in a cloistral habit, Antoine Favray, St Paul Shipwrecked church, Valletta. (courtesy: Stephen Degiorgio)

in this monastery. An intriguing love letter discovered in the archives of the National Library of Malta reveals a 33-year love story between an anonymous man and a certain Sister Giuditta. Indeed, a nun bearing the name of Giuditta Novi lived at the monastery at the time. She died four years after the date of this letter.

Soon after the French invasion of Malta in 1798, the Magdalene monastery was suppressed and the nuns were ordered to leave immediately, taking with them only a few possessions. French soldiers armed with bayonets accompanied them to St Catherine monastery in Republic Street, Valletta. The rest of their precious belongings were seized by the new rulers.

The crypt in St Catherine monastery, Valletta, where the last Magdalenes are interred.

During the Second World War, the monastery was severely damaged by bombing and it was eventually replaced by Valletta's primary school. The Magdalene church survived but for several years it was left in an unkempt state until it was beautifully restored in 2015.

Yet a mystery about this church still waits to be resolved. In 1866, during the construction of an adjacent school, some workers came upon a crypt which appears to be located at the rear of the church. A detailed report by Achille Ferris mentions the refined architectural features of this crypt and the remains of buried nuns within, one of whom was still wearing a habit. Till now, this crypt has not been located.

Opposite: The Orphan Asylum and the Magdalene church, 10 May 1941. (courtesy: Mark Vella, NWMA)

55

COME FULL CIRCLE
Iċ-Ċirku tal-Bidni, Ħaż-Żabbar

At first sight Il-Bidni, at the outskirts of Marsaskala, might seem a peaceful and ordinary rural area off the beaten track. Yet this zone is brimming with mystery, restless to tell its stories to anyone who is interested enough to listen. Tad-Dawl church is a focal point from which one can reach some of these engaging sites.

The first odd structure lies just a few metres away down the church. Locals know it as the Monument of the Three Crosses which has been discussed in a previous article. Some 300 metres away from the church, along Triq il-Bidni and Trejqet Wied ta' Mazza, there is a strange circular field known as Iċ-Ċirku tal-Bidni which has been a source of speculation for many years. The site is privately owned and the public has no access to it. High rubble walls hide it from sight and several adjacent fields make it even more unapproachable.

Some scholars believe that this site was originally an ancient Roman amphitheatre. Well-known writer Alfie Guillaumier mentions this in his *Bliet u Rhula Maltin* and notes that a sculptured head which once decorated this amphitheatre had been unearthed there. A farmer in the area claims that a stone bench which surrounds the circular field is visible in summer when there is no vegetation. Some factors strengthen this theory,

Opposite: The Bidni Circle from the west with Marsaskala Bay in the distance.

Above: The Bidni Circle seen from the west with Ħaż-Żabbar in the background.
Below: The farmhouse that forms part of the perimeter wall and commands the high
ground with views of St Thomas Bay and Birżebbuġa all the way to Ħad-Dingli.

Above: The boundary wall that encloses the depression. Below: The Bidni dolmen and megalithic remains are located a short distance to the east of the circle, behind Tad-Dawl church.

Above: The area immediately to the west of the Bidni Circle.
Opposite: An old photo of the Bidni Circle from the south. (courtesy: Aaron Abela)

such as the high location of this site and the breathtaking views of the countryside and the distant Marsaskala Bay it enjoys – two important elements common in known ancient Roman amphitheatres.

However, this theory has been repudiated by archaeologists who conclude that this is nothing but a doline; a hollow formed by the dissolution of a limestone surface or the collapse of a cave. No archaeological reports seem to be available about the site. Iċ-Ċirku tal-Bidni has been scheduled for its protection by the Planning Authority as a Class B Site of Archaeological Importance and a Grade 2 Site of Scientific Importance.

Interestingly, a Roman villa was known to exist in the Tad-Dawl area. However this archaeological site was destroyed. Nevertheless, around 300 metres away from Iċ-Ċirku tal-Bidni, one finds another archaeological site known as Tal-Bidni Dolmen which is scheduled at Class B. Other megalithic remains are also present in this site. Who knows whether there is any connection between all these finds?

If you have a bizarre story or an
interesting location you would like
to share with the authors,
please get in touch at:
oliver@bdlbooks.com

For more books related to the topics
covered in this publication, go to:
www.bdlbooks.com

Visit our Facebook page:
Bizarre Malta